THE RUMINATOR

THE RUMINATOR

BY

HUMPHREY B. NEILL

A COLLECTION OF THOUGHTS AND SUGGESTIONS ON CONTRARY THINKING

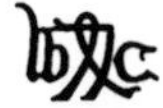

The Caxton Printers, Ltd.
Caldwell, Idaho
2011

Second Printing February 2011

Library of Congress Cataloging in Publication Data

Neill, Humphrey Bancroft, 1895-1977
The Ruminator.

Includes bibliographical references.
1. Securities — United States. 2. Stock-exchange — United States. 3. Speculation. I. Title.
HG4910.N417 332.6320973 73-83115
ISBN 978-0-87004-244-7

Printed and bound in the United States of America by
The Caxton Printers, Ltd.
Caldwell, Idaho 83605
179881

To pry open closed minds and to banish preconceived opinions.

TABLE OF CONTENTS

INTRODUCTION
by Tim Vanech

Last week I went to Barnes and Noble looking for two new books written on the Great Recession of 2008. Surprisingly, these titles were not available in the store. While the employees at the information desk searched their website inventory (unsuccessfully), I went to double check the business section. Instead of the books I was looking for, which must have been considered too technical for mass consumption, I found several bookcases full of shiny offerings in the "personal finance" space. Out of curiosity, I took a Humphrey B. Neill-like stroll around the entire mega store, trolling for a sense of what was most popular with the crowd. Neill believed that if we could follow the growing fascinations of the crowd, and then ruminate and reflect on opposing, contrary perspectives, that we could develop our own minds more fully and independently—that we could be more creative, get closer to a sense of truth, and have a better understanding of the larger forces operating on us and our position within the world.

As I passed through the store aisles, I scanned tables of new releases, coffee table and travel books, cds, dvds, periodicals, the children's section, and obligatory in-store cafe. At the back of the store next to a narrow, standalone bookcase of literary classics, I experienced my epiphany. The best locations at the front of the store, as well as the largest amount of shelf space had all been allocated to books that tell us **how to get rich.**

From my brief, unscientific bookstore browsing, I had confirmed a facile, long-held observation about American culture. We are obsessed with money. More than sex, Hollywood icons, or gossip biographies, star athletes, family dysfunction, recipes, or wellness, it is fear and greed surrounding money that gets us to swipe our credit cards. Despite this national obsession and the accompanying industry that has evolved to profit from it, our skills as a people seem to be weakening when it comes to the acquisition and protection of wealth (exhibit one: the Great Recession of 2008). That must be why we crave books to teach us the basics—the exact steps we need to copy.

And that is just the problem with the approach taken by many of these books. The authors try to share with us the secrets of *others*; how is that rich person's mind wired? They promise to reveal the work of the gurus and masters of money. What do they do that I can't do? Give me a workbook. Give me exercises. I want to know the seven habits, the seven steps, the three pillars of prosperity. Just don't make me think for myself—or about myself. I want to *do* something, *anything*. Give me something to do, so I can be an American money ninja like those tanned shouters on CNBC.

Maybe the problem is that these experts espouse so many ways of enriching themselves, I mean, us, that it becomes overwhelming to choose only one path. One author guarantees success if we buy foreclosure properties. Rich Dad Kiyosaki tells us that being a lifelong employee is the road to financial ruin. Another guru tells us that he has a magic formula for identifying cheap stocks at the push of a few virtual internet buttons, while yet another proffers a methodology utilizing fixed, guaranteed insurance products as the way to *financial independence*—a term that always reminds me of "Depends," those adult diapers. David Bach tells us if we just grind our own cheap, coffee beans and avoid buying lattes at Starbucks, then we can "automatically" become like our rich, unassuming neighbor with the old truck and worn Sears khaki pants who lives like a hermit with his staycations, Costco runs, his Quicken reports, and perfectly integrated, online investment plan. You can almost hear a low toned chant through this aisle of books in praise of dollar cost averaging.

I admit that I am no different in that I am also obsessed with money. I am a money manager by nature and training, and I would bet very few of my friends and clients would argue that I should be doing something else. I am passionate about my work, and hopefully I have gained a bit more financial skill than someone who does something more balanced for a living. However, much of what I know has not been learned from books but from listening to my clients' words, by observing their behavior and life choices with regard to money—and then stopping to consider what I have seen and heard. There is deep value in a look inside oneself, self-reflection if you will, as well as a look at the facts, a simple approach that has become lost by thought-flooded, anxious Americans. Although I poke fun at our ill-fated grasps at security or riches, it is a gallows humor that I should not let mask my true concern for the personal financial challenges we all face.

At one time, I had spent a couple of years writing a draft of a book to help people invest better from their own wisdom in a world without guarantees. But the business of writing what was going to be yet another self-help financial book became tedious and removed from actually providing something of use. It isn't about the information or methodology that you can convey, it is about the method of conveyance and the audience to which you wish to communicate. You need a catchy system, the editor said, to deliver a specific number of steps, and workbook exercises at the conclusion of each chapter. You need to give readers something to do, something to fill in or complete. Oh, and a book like this today is more easily published if you have a platform. That means you need to have a website with unique users who you can count and then guarantee will buy the book. They wanted to know what "markets" I was after. Corporate executives? Financial planners and advisors? The mass affluent (moderately rich)? Or dysfunctional debtors (middle class and lower)?

Financial publishers these days want a multi-media star, someone to get on television, radio, (now it would be to tweet and to Facebook too), and to get out there on the road offering seminars, maybe work the minor leagues at an event headlined by Trump at an Expo Center. I sensed I would need whitened teeth, darkened hair, and speech coaching while subsisting on fish and weeds swallowed with spring water in airport lounges between flights and sets of abdominal work-outs. I wouldn't have had the conviction or stamina to sustain such a career leap, let alone the required regimen of tanning my skin.

Over those two years of thinking, writing, and some agonizing self-reflection, I learned that I was like the boy protagonist at the conclusion of James Joyce's great short story, "Araby," who sees himself as "a creature driven and derided by vanity." Rather than pursue a vault to my fated constellation or a flight by the sun, I came to realize that I was going to do my best for my clients and their families, the ones who had placed their trust in me, those few who seemed to appreciate what I was offering. My newsletters became my small and quiet versions of what Bruce Springsteen did with *Thunder Road*, his invitation to the world to come on a journey with him, when he began to develop his adult voice and knew that he wanted to connect with an audience about his observations, his beliefs, and his characters—his people. Like William Carlos William in Paterson, NJ, my search for meaning would have to come from the daily work of my practice, from a life lived, which would provide the kind of ongoing communication and mutual growth that I needed to sustain myself, my clients, and, hopefully, my family.

It was through my own newsletters that Al Neill, son of Humphrey B. Neill, and I became acquainted. Al showed me around his family's old Vermont farmhouse. He described his father as having had a "peppery" personality with no formal college education but an insatiable curiosity to learn. This hunger for knowledge is evinced by the various rooms in the home that were converted to studies over the years. As if the house were not large enough to contain this passion, Humphrey B. Neill ran out of space for his books after converting yet another room, an upstairs bathroom in this case, to a small library and went out to the barn to build and fill more bookcases. Throughout his writings, Neill, like a cheerful Sherpa or curious, distinctly American philosopher and teacher, provides suggested texts to his readers for further study, gestures that would be hard to envision being made by today's popular financial writers.

During the first of my stays, I occupied Humphrey B. Neill's main study, also doubling as an upstairs bedroom, the walls lined with full bookcases from floor to ceiling. There I read through Neill's own newsletters and correspondence with money managers as luminary as Ed Johnson II of Fidelity fame and fortune. Johnson personally held a subscription to Neill's *Letters of Contrary Opinion* as did several of his colleagues when the firm created one of Fidelity's flagship funds, the *Contrafund*, based on Neill's contrary approach. At that time, Fidelity as an entire firm managed about $3 billion dollars. Humphrey B. Neill apparently held the first share of *Contrafund*, a fund that in May of 2010 managed over $65 billion in assets.

Al Neill explained to me how gratified his father was to have readers far and wide, readers of the highest education who subscribed to his *Neill Letters of Contrary Opinion.* To stimulate further discussion and debate, his father held popular forums in Vermont each fall where Wall Street big-boys and individual contrary folk from various backgrounds gathered to improve their thinking on various topics of interest and concern. To this day there still exists a famous Contrarian investment conference in Vermont, a land that seems natural for the practice of going against the grain of accepted or budding conventional wisdoms.

Humphrey B. Neill's work, by its very nature, its proposed observation of crowd formation behavior and counsel to think contrarily in order to be better informed, is resistant to the type of mass popularity evident in the financial books of today. And that engrained marginality is what makes Neill's way of seeing the world and being in it so helpful today. As William Blake wrote, "Wisdom is sold in the desolate market where none come to buy." Well, some have come to buy Neill's *Art of Contrary Thinking;* it has remained in print for more than 50 years gathering significance and relevance.

The rigor and curiosity evident in Neill's writings fill the void for a reader hungry for understanding or a way to think through the dizzying 24 hour cable news cycles and the attendant, superficial sensationalism that bombard us in modern life. Think of the sound bites, more like efficient blasts utilized to impact our fears around Y2K, SARS, 9/11, the 2000 tech wreck, or the Meltdown of 2008 that oozed into March, 2009 causing pundits to predict that an appetite for stocks would never return. (The Dow then rose from about 6,500 to 11,200, a gain of more than 70% in about 13 months.) Do you remember the feel of the gathering mass opinion surrounding each of those events? Neill warns us of the inherent wrongness of crowds at extreme moments.

In addition to our fears, Neill also teaches us how to limit the damage we can do ourselves through greed and our human proclivity toward mania. Do you remember when marketers sold us the idea that oat bran was the cure-all making its way into our cereal, crackers, bread, and bagels? Where is oat bran now? Relegated to a few specialty products in the bread aisle? Think about our ongoing national obsession with low fat diets. There was a time when everyone seemed to eat bagels, which had almost no fat, while swilling diet drinks hand over fist in an effort to combat the "bulge". Soon after, Dr. Atkins taught us that those bagels were full of evil carbohydrates and showed us how to live thinly in an insulin-shocked state of starvation eating meat plates intermittently like ravenous cavemen while avoiding said carbs as if they were poisonous mushrooms. I remember the plummet of stocks related to pasta and bread. Those companies survived and thrived once more as has obesity and financial ignorance.

Neill believed that a large and quickly gathering mass of opinion provided the perfect backdrop for the most accurate counterarguments. One of the most successful money managers of our current time, Jeremy Grantham, has focused his firm's research on bubbles, how to capitalize on them when they begin to form but to be long gone when they pop. Like Neill, Grantham knows that when hot money, like hot air, comes whooshing in, there are a variety of other investments that don't receive the capital they deserve from the supposedly efficient marketplace. Today one thinks of China and gold as magnets for money, but what other long term trends and ideas lie in the shadows, underpriced, less risky, and ripe for the investor connected to the pulse of the universe but not driven mad by its pounding in his ears. Neill cautioned against our predilection for prediction and claimed that his contrarian methodology was not after accurate forecasts per se; instead, he focused on probable anticipations, which were often borne from following opposite thinking to mainstream ideas.

Can you imagine what Neill would have thought of Larry Kudlow on CNBC pushing his guests to say in one word (because the advertisements need to run) whether the market would be up or down in 6 months? Or even better, to give old Larry a number where the Dow will be at year-end?

I have marveled at Neill's prescience in writing, sixty years ago, on the possible role of space in politics and commerce in years to come—this long before missile defense systems, cell phones, and satellites. It made sense to Neill decades ago that China's socialism would move toward capitalism and that our own democratic capitalism would become more socialized. Neill also provides a step by step analysis on how governments who wish to go to war prepare their case and go about manipulating the masses into the required support. As I read his work written decades before I was alive, visions of Colin Powell, Dick Cheney, and George Bush came into my mind—apparently the most recent version of an archetypal procedure. How accurate and helpful such thinking is to our sense of understanding.

In Neill's writing, we witness a methodology for understanding through internal argument, for becoming freer and more independent thinkers, and we see the author's own example on the page, his sustained drive for accuracy and truth. We have a history of this ethic in America. Thomas Paine argued in *Common Sense* that if you wanted to learn something of value, then you had better teach yourself. In Benjamin Franklin's autobiography, we learn about the man, but we also get numerous practical tips to improve ourselves, further detailed in his *Way to Wealth*. (One might argue that F. Scott Fitzerald's modernist reprise to Franklin's daily routine is the poignant boyhood diary of Gatsby, born James Gatz, as he develops a hollow identity and an unmoored pursuit of wealth and Daisy). New England Transcendentalists like Thoreau and Emerson (in *Self-Reliance*) embraced alternate, contrary ways of finding meaning and truth in our lives; they wrote about the importance of an introspective, personal search even as they attempted to create a national cultural identity in contrast to England's. We are, in part, a culture (admirably so) of self-help traditions, Western pioneers, seekers of salvation through craftsmanship as opposed to an Old World indentured servitude. This creates in us a real weakness for quacks, marketers, and snake oil salesmen like those shysters in Mark Twain's *The Adventures of Huckleberry Finn*.

The popular finance books of today, and the marketing departments of their publishers exaggerate and caricature, if not manipulate, our cultural vulnerability for self improvement. In our nation of the self-made, we learn from F. Scott Fitzgerald's Gatsby about the seductive possibilities of our capitalist system as well as the dark hangover, the unmooring of the soul that occurs when forming an identity divorced from heart, meaning, and authenticity.

Thirty five years after *The Great Gatsby* was published, Walker Percy wrote *The Moviegoer* in a post-Korean War 1962. Percy was termed an American existentialist. His protagonist, Binx Bolling, a stockbroker in New Orleans, begins the novel adrift and "spinning down the coast" in his fancy convertible with various pretty secretaries who come and go. Bolling suffers from a case of what he terms "the malaise," a kind of modernist haze, born from chaos and war, the diluting effect of secularism on religion, of Americanism on tradition. Untethered and free, Binx tries to escape the malaise, in dark movie theaters in the play of light, pictures, and faint romance; he notes the rising need for Americans to validate their hometowns by seeing them appear on television. When Binx finds a woman, Kate, to care for, he realizes that sometimes we just need a good "kick in the ass," that meaning is born from the search. He believes that if you are not on a search, that you have nothing and are nowhere. Ultimately, the character finds meaning and fulfillment in finding footholds in life and "handing one another along," that is connecting to others and helping them for "good and selfish reasons."

Humphrey B. Neill writes on this side of our better nature—in the impulse of the earliest Americans like Thomas Paine and Benjamin Franklin, who wanted to help their common citizens think for themselves, the Transcendentalists like Thoreau and Emerson, and with an awareness of Modernism and Existentialism of his own lifetime. The steps, recipes, and workbooks of today's finance books would have been silly to Neill, certainly antithetical to the thinking process he believed would help people. He did not seek the status analogous to today's multi-platform, mega-marketing star, the guru, which creates in consumers a fruitless search for a priest as opposed to God or wisdom or peace.

Without false promises, Neill reveals to us that we can think and succeed ourselves, and his work reminds us that "ruminating" and cogitating on the volatility of the world can make us *feel* better through understanding the ebbs and flows of group thinking and mass psychology—while not having to react to everything and by decreasing errors we might make in investments or life through too fast conclusions. For those of us who manage money, we know how powerful it is to be wrong less often.

It is important to note that Neill refers to contrary thinking as an "art," decidedly not a science. For most of us, it's not easy to accept that thinking effectively on life, investments, and our own happiness is a work of creativity. It's hard because we are not used to it—that we need to search and to be open and perhaps to build our own lists, as opposed to following someone else's. It takes a long time to feel like we're making progress and is a continuous process of balance and footholds against a mountain of challenges. I have learned this in my own life, from my most prosperous clients, who are creative, contrary and often entrepreneurial, common people doing uncommon and personally suitable things that others would not try. Neill knew that over time and with persistence, wisdom would come, but it would come from within, not from without—in opposition to the crowd.

Humphrey B. Neill was most interested in "the human side of the market," and it is clear that he was a pioneer in the rapidly evolving behavioral finance subset of economics. We know now that people and markets are *not* rational in the here and now, and we'd better pay attention to human behavior if we want to progress in our thinking. Neill was also one of our first contrarians, a now overused and misunderstood moniker. So it is enormously helpful to return to the original source, here in Neill's work, and to understand the contrarian's simultaneous connection to the tides of humanity as well as the necessary self-protection in constructing contrary positions. His defense of individualism—our ability to develop a sense of proportion and common sense, to cultivate a rational long term view or one from high above—reminds me of yet another uniquely American moment in literature. In Ralph Ellison's *Invisible Man,* written in 1953 around the time of the first edition of Neill's *Art of Contrary Thinking,* the unnamed narrator tells us that "on the lower frequencies," he speaks for us, the readers, those who will listen. And this is where we find the simple wisdom of a self-made Vermonter who offers us a hand with our worries and concerns, who teaches us to teach ourselves, guidance for those of us who accept the invitation.

> Let us occasionally put aside speculation and market worries. When we do get away from them, they become dwarfed and lose their disturbing aspect.
>
> I am writing this in the shade of a hundred-and-twenty-five-year-old Vermont maple, and can look through its massive branches to green pastures beyond. A delightful, century-old house and neighborly barns somehow bring a quieting philosophy, and a peaceful perspective upon the problems of Wall Street. We need to get away frequently in order to realize that market fluctuations are not the all-important facts in life. If "business leaders" would desert their conferences, their gold clubs, Rotary Clubs, and merger meetings, and run away from everything, deep into the country, I am sure that they themselves would be

happier, as well as make our business lives pleasanter and more evenly tempered. It does little good to leave Wall Street for summer resorts where stock tickers and business gossip continue. If you do go away, get beyond the fringe of advertising billboards and chambers of commerce. Seek the woods and hills; visit the villages where bread and butter are earned by the sweat of the brow, and where, evenings and Sundays, you join in good fellowship with your neighbors instead of in worship of the Almighty Dollar.

—from Neill's Tape Reading and Market Tactics (1931-original publication, 1959—special reprint)

Tim Vanech, a contemporary contrarian, is a founder and Managing Director of Shorepoint Capital Partners LLC, a registered investment advisor and wealth management firm, in Stoughton, MA. He has over 15 years of financial services experience. Prior to that, he served as a Head Teaching Fellow at Harvard University, where he studied with McArthur Award and Pulitzer Prize winner Robert Coles. Tim earned Certificates of Distinction in Teaching in each of his three years. His letter on equity risk and valuation was featured in the December 2007 issue of *Barron's*. He also holds a A. B. *cum laude* in English and American Literature from Harvard University and has done graduate work in Creative Writing. His short story "White Flight" was published by W. W. Norton in *25 and Under/Fiction* and he also published fiction in *Doubletake* magazine. He lives in Canton, MA, with his wife, daughter and son.

FOREWORD

IN THIS second volume on the subject of Contrary Opinions and their usefulness in business and financial thinking and decision-making, let me quote a paragraph from the foreword of *The Art of Contrary Thinking* (first published by Caxton 20 years ago):

> The art of contrary thinking consists in training your mind to ruminate in directions opposite to general public opinions; and to weigh your conclusions in the light of current events and current manifestations of human behavior.

During a large share of the years — years of emotional turmoil — from 1968 to 1973, it was this writer's pleasurable task to write and issue a small monthly publication titled *The Ruminator — A Periodical of Perspective.* (Contrary ruminating leads to broadened perspectives.) This was in addition to the "Neill Letters of Contrary Opinion," which have been published by the writer on a fortnightly basis for the past 25 years.

The little journal permitted an informal approach to the subjects under review not possible in a tightly written "newsletter" often composed against time. It was most pleasing when the publisher of my former book, The Art of Contrary Thinking, became interested in a further "collection of thoughts and suggestions on contrary thinking," as presented in the following reprints of articles from the monthly journals.

Permit me to stress one point in connection with these discussions: these were written in a period of America's greatest emotional turmoil of the century, if not of its nearly 200 years of existence as a Republic. I find in going over these comments, that they bring back in focus this era with its numerous shocks and crises this nation (and you and I) stood up against in this recent period. The only revisions in the text were those needed for clarifying the time elements, some tenses shifted, and a word or two changed to fit the context.

HUMPHREY B. NEILL

Saxton River, Vermont
February, 1974

THE RUMINATOR

THE "WHY" AND THE "HOW" OF THE CONTRARY THEORY

ACTING the wrong way, and at the wrong time, is a routine common to Wall Street. The purpose of contrary opinions is to avoid the predictions that go wrong, notably in the stock market.

Why it pays to be contrary has been amply demonstrated through the years. Only lately, the toboggan-year in 1966, and the roller coaster in 1969-70, were anything but "fun" years. Contrary action in January, 1966, and again in October, made fortunes for contra-acting speculators. Likewise, contrarians preserved their egos and protected their capital during the bitter 18 months from January, 1969 to June 1970, as also many did during 1973.

History repeatedly illustrates the value of when to "go opposite" to the Crowd. (The Crowd is not *always* wrong, by the way.)

Has everyone forgotten the shattered dreams of the great Florida Land Boom, of the 1920's, that led to the extravaganza in Wall Street in 1929? (We were told in 1929 that the nation was perched upon "a plateau of permanent prosperity.")

Who has forgotten the Performance Game of more recent experience? Thought to make everyone rich, many found their pocketbooks badly bent by bad performances.

For some 30 months after the Cambodian Panic, of May, 1970, bullish contrarians held the advantage. They recognized socio-political and economic changes that resulted in revival.

It is axiomatic, if you stop to think about it, that when everyone is bearish, or bullish, the force of the price-momentum is broken.

It takes time to become a contrarian, to learn to "think in reverse." The purpose of *The Ruminator* is to discuss "how" one may become a successful contrarian. The question comprises People and Opinions; both can be provocative.

Even after the many years I have written on the Theory of Contrary Opinion I continue to receive inquiries, asking "What is the idea of contrary opinion anyway?" Also, there are those who doubt the theory has validity. Surely, we have shown over the years that there is a lot more than "fuzz" in being contrary. It is a winning mental process for those who work at it.

HOW TO KEEP FROM GUESSING WRONG

Be A Non-Conformist When Using Your Mind

In the fewest possible words, the above states the idea of my Theory of Contrary Opinion. Be a nonconformist in the use of your mind; when everyone thinks alike, everybody is likely to be wrong.

To present the idea behind the theory let me describe it under two heads: People and Opinions.

The Theory is based upon the oldest of human traits — traits which show up as our emotions are aroused: fear, greed, hope, pride-of-opinion, wishful-thinking and others.

Our emotions, in turn, are affected and acted upon by *imitation* and *contagion.* These are the two culprits most responsible for conformity and sameness of thinking. (For a play on words, note that imitation and contagion are accountable for uncountable wrong decisions.)

Another mental habit that is often our ruination, when we hope to make wise decisions, is preconceived opinions. Here we have the real rival to contrary opinions. Preconceived opinions leave little room in our minds for contrary viewpoints. One of the reasons it is difficult for security analysts to become working contrarians is that their analytical studies tend to formulate set, or pre-conceived opinions. However, analysts will find contrary ideas useful to check their findings.

Thus, to sum up this far, while the traits that account for the success in contrary thinking are old and known to everyone, the idea of thinking contrarily is a neglected art (which I ventured to remedy in my book, *The Art of Contrary Thinking*).

The Crowd And The Popular Mind

As stated, our subject entails people and opinions. Let us now discuss "whom we go contrary to" in our thinking and acting.

Everyone knows what a crowd is, but few recognize the significance of Crowd Psychology, or have much conception of what Le Bon termed the "popular mind." From this Ruminator's long experience in observing "the crowd in action," it is demonstrable that a study of the Crowd Mind will prevent costly errors in forecasting.

There are various types of crowds, both miscellaneous and distinctive. We are not concerned here with the ordinary groupings of people — such as hurrying crowds on the streets or those pushing their way into subways, crowds at a football game or on their days off at the beach.

Suppose we classify the crowds we are interested in:

Miscellaneous Crowds — those made up of various groups, especially Consumers. For our analysis, we wish to know what the millions are thinking about who eat up and use up the products of industry and the farm; what their opinions are. In attempting to judge socio-economic and political conditions, we are vitally concerned with the trend of thought among this vast hoard of spenders. (This is an essential link in monetary analysis.) Consumers, needless to add, embrace business, industry, and agriculture too, not simply householders.

Distinctive or Sub-Crowds are those groups which have similar interests. For instance, you may wish to ruminate over the opinions expressed by bankers in regard to monetary conditions, interest rates, and so on. The trader in the stock market certainly pays attention to what the "crowd" of Fund Managers appears to be doing, and what they are thinking about. Fund managers wield a tremendous force in the stock market; their operations reach into the hundreds of millions of dollars. They tend to act as a crowd.

Then, too, the ever-expanding number of analysts, advisers, and financial commentators require especial concentration, because their words and forecasts are bandied about until the influence becomes greater than might be supposed. It is well to obtain an occasional consensus of advisory service and brokers' opinions, so you will know what these professional prognosticators are talking about.* Quite frequently they become of one mind in their opinions, strange as it may seem. When they do, it usually pays to be contra-minded. These crowds of stock-market-minded experts are highly influential.** Today with the Analyst Societies, we have access to Wall Street opinions; we can keep track of the professional crowd-mind.

This is a good place to stress that in our survey of opinions, for the purpose of considering contrary viewpoints (and contrary action), a Crowd is a Crowd, whether amateur or professional. A group of pros can become as one-sided in their opinions, and in their activities, as a bunch of neophites. Anybody can get carried away with their emotions — unless they have trained themselves to take time for some contrary thoughtfulness.

The Popular Mind: When we speak of the "popular mind" the reference is to what is in the crowd's mind. You might refer to it in the expression, Group Think, or think-

---

* For a fortnightly appraisal of advisory-service opinions see Investors Intelligence, published in Larchmont, N.Y. 10538. This bulletin checks 74 services and reports on the resulting ratio of bulls to bears, plus the undecideds. It is a very helpful guide to the way the advisory Crowd is thinking.

** For a comprehensive survey of the financial services industry (it has become a larger one than generally supposed) see an excellent Critique by Robert T. Gross, President of Lynatrace, Inc., 4000 N.E. Third Ave., Pompano Beach, Fla. 33064; also see story of the industry by Dana Thomas in Barron's Weekly of September 4, 1972. (This writer appears in both.)

ing alike. Thus we come to the factor of conformity. People like to conform with one another. They think alike, they eat alike, they play alike, they like to be in crowds. Groups dress alike. Where the crowd goes others follow.

Take traders in the stock market. Their charts induce conformity, as they are all looking at the same lines or X's on the graphs. Additionally, they read the same financial news and scan similar advisory sheets. Unless he is contrary, a speculator, or an investor, finds the tug of sameness almost too much to resist. He conforms to the Group Mind. Thus it is that "everybody" becomes bullish or bearish together.

The characteristics of crowds vary as crowds themselves do. Yet, a Crowd is impulsive. People in crowds will do things, and say things, they probably would not think of doing, if alone with their thoughts. An individual differs from a Crowd in many respects, especially in that the emotional impact of the crowd mind is not bearing down upon him.

A dictum by Johann Schiller, 18th Century philosopher, poet and dramatist (and colleague of Goethe's), illustrates the foregoing comment. "Anyone taken as an individual," wrote Schiller, "is tolerably sensible and reasonable — as a member of a crowd, he at once becomes a blockhead." (This bon mot was unearthed by Bernard Baruch and is found in his foreword to the reprint edition of Mackay's indispensable book for contrarians: *Extraordinary Popular Delusions and the Madness of Crowds.*)

Let me emphasize that crowd-sentiment — how the crowd "feels" and "acts" may evolve and ripen without the crowd being assembled together.

Visualize thousands of businessmen or speculators sitting in their homes or offices catching up on their reading. Before them are large circulation news-letters, bank bulletins, economic reviews, weekly financial magazines, plus brokers' and advisory-service reports. Unconsciously, the majority will soon be of a similar mind. They will be a crowd "in thought," if not in person.

WHERE DO "OPINIONS" SPRING FROM? WHO CREATES THEM? WHAT CREATES THEM?

Mass Opinions are created by Opinion Leaders, by sudden events, by happenings, by mass communication, by propaganda — and by imitation and contagion.

Numerous tests and polis indicate that reinforcement of prior opinions is more commonly accomplished by mass communications than is conversion from one viewpoint to an opposing one. (Joseph T. Klapper reports on this and other aspects of the receptivity of the Crowd in his *The Effects of Mass Communication.*)

Another point Klapper refers to is that "ideas often flow from radio (television) and print to the opinion leaders and from them to the less active sections of the population." Opinion Leaders are a most active source of general opinions. Their expressed viewpoints and arguments are always under observation by studious contrarians. The Opinion Leaders one pays especial attention to, of course, are those in the fields one is particularly concerned with. A stock-market speculator gives heed to prominent Wall Streeters and commentators whose influence affects the movements of stock prices. In politics, he follows the activities and speeches of those who sway voters, those who support or oppose legislation he is interested in, and those who are the "king makers" and political Opinion Leaders.

I cannot overstress the importance of heeding these "makers of opinions" because through the force and momentum of contagion (of ideas) and imitation (of "leaders") sentiment can become well entrenched among the masses.

Sudden events quickly crystallize opinions. An unexpected stock-market break of sharp proportions can shift opinions overnight from indifference or optimism to fear and distrust. In fashions, style shows and publications create fads as Social Leaders pose with their gowns and other wearables.

As for locating and measuring printed opinions to counter-check, let me outline how I go about it. A similar method may accommodate other readers.

In order to run down popular notions and the voluminous output of predictions, comments and advice that influence the public's opinions and their actions, I spend a great deal of time scanning and reading various publications, in addition to listening over radio and television.

It is possible to get a "feel" of how general opinions are running by taking note of comments and headlines, by skimming editorial writers and columnists for slants and indications of current interest, and by reviewing news-letters, speeches and interviews. (Advertising, too, requires attention.)

Below are a number of publications to which, among others, I pay regular attention. You can add more, but these few give a broad coverage of standard, conventional viewpoints in the field of finance, economics, Wall Street, and socio-political trends. The last-named trends are enormously effective on Crowd sentiment and feelings, which in turn influence decisions and actions.

What to seek are publications that quote what various leaders, commentators and groups are saying. Look for consensus reports from significant gatherings and forums. One thereby receives a cross-section of majority opinion on important questions of the moment: prospects for coming elections, the judgments of those who comment on the war or current domestic events, as well as the views of editors, prominent columnists, financiers, and industrialists. Try these publications: —

U.S. News & World Report — Business Week, —Barron's —Time — Newsweek, — Wall Street Journal — Journal of Commerce — Metropolitan Daily Newspapers and Trade Journals.

Because of the wide range of references and quotes, the above give one a fair sampling of general opinions and prevailing sentiment in the country. You will be able to keep track of significant predictions, as they are released by Trade Associations, Economic Seminars and other groups. I simply list a group of publications that will give a workable "consensus."

It is extraordinary, but not unusual to find comments in such publications surprisingly similar in content and viewpoint. I have often remarked that one would suppose the editors of this voluminous branch of literature gathered in an immense hall and compared notes, in order to formulate standard comments and predictions.

Is not habitual conformity in thinking to be expected from this sameness of opinions?

I have sloganized it this way: When writers write alike, readers are likely to think alike.

From the standpoint of adopting contrary opinions as a protection against conformity, let me add that the more universal one finds popular opinions the more he may rely upon a counter analysis.

Opinions have to be continually checked for their "fickleness." At one moment we may note popular acceptance of some question, only to see interest in it die almost immediately.

Another instance of the fickleness of opinions is noted when "trial balloons" are sent aloft to get the public's reaction to someone's ideas or schemes that he wishes to promote or desires to test out.

In reading and skimming for common viewpoints, and for prevailing sentiment, what we are after in particular is a trend in the commentaries and news that is likely to lead to contagious action; that which will catch the Crowd's fancy and be imitated.

I mentioned advertising. You sense from the advertising of brokers and advisory services how they feel — and therefore probably how they are writing in their advices and recommendations. One can see behind the headlines whether they are bullish or bearish. Often, indeed, they express their views openly in their ads.

Barron's Weekly and the Sunday *New York Times* carry a large amount of advertising of brokers and advisory services. When a contrarian notes that advertising of advisory services swamps the pages he recognizes it is time to move very cautiously. Heavy advertising obviously indicates the Crowd is eager for tips and advice, and is itching to trade, if not already actively trading in the market. A dearth of advertising indicates the opposite.

Finally, to be a practicing contrarian requires diligent "ruminating on the strange mutability of human affairs," to give you my favorite quote from Dicken's inimitable Mr. Pickwick (who in turn gave me my title of *The Ruminator).*

CROWD PSYCHOLOGY, THE MISSING LINK

Although more attention is paid to public and crowd psychology today than in previous eras, it still remains the missing link in economic and financial commentaries and forecasts.

What people think and do are, in the final analysis, the primary forces in a free society.

People can be influenced, the Crowd can be swayed and panicked, but what counts is the action that takes place.

In our practice of Contrary Opinions, I urge that more emphasis be given to "what everyone does." What everyone thinks about is not enough.

When everybody acts alike, their actions are often wrong.

This may be illustrated in mob scenes and riots, of course, but wrong actions by the public frequently occur in ordinary, harmless pursuits, such as when the Crowd rushes into the stock market just before a collapse in prices.

Studies of *activities* in which the public is emotionally interested as well as *notions* that people hold, come within our studies of why contrary opinions are so frequently the *right* opinions.

For example, here are some queries that are pertinent to various periods and events:

> Are people spending normally, abnormally, or holding back? Are savings a higher percentage of spendable incomes than customary? From such questions, we get a sense of the public's activities, as well as of their opinions.
>
> How will people vote? Will there be a large "undecided" proportion of voters in the polis just before election day?
>
> How are Wall Street groups acting; is the public actively in the market?

The Theory of Contrary Opinion is predicated upon appraisals of one-sided viewpoints. Thus we have to analyze the consensus of this or that "crowd." (There may be any number of crowds engaged in varying activities or having divergent opinions.)

At this point, I am merely stressing that what the Crowd does (with its money, for instance) is of significance, as is what the one-sided majority is thinking about.

What Makes People Follow The Crowd?

In both thinking and doing, with both opinions and actions, the psychological pressures from contagion and imitation are constantly in effect, so the majority commonly follows the Crowd.

Contagion and imitation play on the human emotions of hope, fear, greed and pride-of-opinion. They beget a response from the Crowd that a Leonard Bernstein acquires from a symphony orchestra. "A symphony of agreement."

Frequently over the years I have referred to contagion and imitation. They are actually the basis for "being contrary," because of their influence on opinions and emotions.

An authoritative source of information on "imitation" is Gabriel Tarde's celebrated *The Laws of Imitation.*

Gabriel Tarde was Professor of Modern Philosophy in the College of France. "A born student of human nature, M. Tarde was from the first interested in that oldest of philosophical problems, the explanation of motive," according to the introduction.

In the preface to the second edition (1895), Professor Tarde wrote:

> "There are two ways of imitating; namely, to act exactly like one's model, or to do exactly the contrary.
>
> "Hence the necessity of those divergences which Spencer points out, without explaining, in his law of progressive differentiation. Nothing can be affirmed without suggesting, no matter how simple the social environment, not only the idea that is affirmed but the negation of this idea as well.
>
> "This is the reason why the affirmation of idealism gives birth to the idea of materialism; why the establishment of monarchy engenders the idea of republicanism, etc.
>
> "Let us say, then, from the wider point of view, that a society is a group of people who display many resemblances produced either by imitation or by *counter-imitation.*"

Leaving imitation for the present, let me touch on contagion sufficiently to complete the thought process that might have been set up in your mind when the subject was introduced above.

I mentioned "a symphony of agreement," when referring to Crowds. Another favorite mentor of mine, in the development of my Theory of Contrary Opinion, has been another Frenchman, Gustav Le Bon, author of *The Crowd – A Study of the Popular Mind.* Le Bon refers to the -mental unity of crowds," in his psychological studies of the popular mind.

Le Bon stresses *contagion* as a primary characteristic of crowd behavior.

Contagion occurs — and is extremely effective — not only when crowds assemble — but also when some new thought, program, fad or movement presents itself. It may "catch" and become widespread in a matter of days.

What psychologists call "suggestibility" is a form of contagion. Also, the power of suggestion may cause a contagious spread of some idea, fad, notion or popular movement.

O.P.M. Operators In The Stock Market

The contrast in type among the big operators in Wall Street today, with those of 45-50 years ago, is most significant.

The difference is so important, for the effect on fluctuations and trends, that every contrarian who speculates in the market will have it in mind constantly. How operators work has startling force on stock movements — perhaps on the very stock our contrary speculator is playing with. It is one of the changes the Contrary Theory deals with.

The difference may be summed up by saying today's operators that hit the headlines, and are making the killings, and the losings, are operating with other people's money. I use the initials, O.P.M., to attract your attention.

Let us go back to the great speculative boom of 45 years ago. In the years 1928 and 1929 the Wall Streeters who made the headlines because of their speculative successes were of two classes.

First, there were those who played with their own money exclusively (Jesse Livermore might be used for an illustration; or Bernard Baruch in earlier years). There were many very successful market operators who made lots of money, although the majority lost their pile in the crash, and disappeared from the news.

The second group were what were known as pool managers.- These were the extra-smart operators who not only traded with their own funds, but with those of associates. However, the pool operator had his own money at stake, as well as his friends' — which is the point I wish to make. He was susceptible to the strains of risking his own money.

Note now how the millionaires make it today.

In a word, it is "institutional" money that is being used today, to make millions for clever operators. By use of the word *institutional* I include *funds* of all types, including mutual funds.

In a *Business Week* story several very successful young operators, of this modern school, were written up (Dec.

30, 1967 — "The Young Millionaires of Finance"). It is worth reading in order to see how they work and how they earn their keep.

You may be asking yourself, "what difference whose money is used, so long as the guy knows what he's doing and does it successfully?"

There is all the difference in the world. We can state it briefly, in two parts:

1. By using money other than his own, the operator is in large degree free of the emotional stymie that causes the average person "to do the wrong thing at the wrong time." We have all experienced losses by doing what we knew all along we shouldn't do! We weren't contrary!

2. When the great spills occur — as in 1962, 1966, 1969, or in any slide-off you care to mention — our OPM operator need not do what the frightened individual on margin is forced to do, or what the pool operator had to do — that is, frantically sell. The funds can ride through the storm; the operator may feed bad, but he hasn't lost his money; the "asset value" slumps, but so have the figures for other funds and institutions.

Competition among fund managers is keen. The result has been active switching of shares. Also, let me add, many funds have made unusual records for their stock.

The Franchise Craze And Puckle's Machine Company

Don't get the idea I am about to downgrade the franchise business. Not when one hears about things like Kentucky Fried Chicken which was a bonanza for a lot of people. Dunkin' Donuts, recently offered by a leading group of investment bankers and brokers, started out in a lively fashion, also.

Nevertheless, the craze for "franchises" assuredly is subject for mention and rumination by contrarians. If you have been a regular reader of the Wall Street Journal, you have noticed the extraordinary amount of advertising space that has been, and is, given over to locating prospects for various types of franchises.

In looking over the ads in the Journal I could not resist turning to the famous list of "bubble companies" contained in Mackay's famous book, *Extraordinary Popular Delusions and the Madness of Crowds.* In his chapter titled "The South Sea Bubble," the author names over 85 promotions that were organized at the time the South Sea Company was originated by the Harley Earl of Oxford, in 1711.

I picked on Puckle's Machine Company to add to our story, merely because it sounds like an exciting venture! It seems the organizers planned to manufacture a machine for discharging round and square cannon-balls and bullets, thereby revolutionizing the art of war. It was caricatured in this bit of verse:

> "A rare invention to destroy the crowd
> Of fools at home instead of fools abroad,
> Fear not, my friends, this terrible machine,
> They're only wounded who have shares therein."

I remind you that another "game" of the late era shortly came a cropper. That is, the idea of trying to catch stock offerings as they come out of registration, in hopes of getting in on one of those "hot issues" that double the first day. This sort of get-rich-quick activity can never work very long, but it's fun while it lasts. The average trader usually finds it impossible, however, to obtain shares in these new issues. Incidentally, they tell me that Dunkin' Donuts was one of these double-uppers when it came out. A mouthwatering morsel!

No one would suppose that we would witness a Bubble Era in these enlightened decades of the 20th Century!

It is not a specific company that I am ruminating about, but about the way varying types of investment fads become highly contagious. As the crowds gather, the risks increase. The conglomerate cult was another illustration. Gold and silver are the bonanzas as this book goes to press.

FOLKWAYS: HOW FOLKS ACT

A big book was written around the turn of the century, that has a warm title: "Folkways." How much more friendly this sounds — actually, how much more comprehensive it sounds — than if it were titled principles of sociology, which it covers most understandingly.

Oldtimers will doubtless remember the author, William Graham Sumner, who was a great supporter of the American free-enterprise system, a most popular professor at Yale, and an outstanding authority on social customs, mores and morals. This particular book (he wrote many others, including a delightful essay on "The Forgotten Man") was commenced in 1899.

Folkways, or the customs and ways of people, are obviously the basis for the theory of Contrary Opinion. Accordingly, we can learn from such authorities as Professor Sumner, who fortunately had the gift of making his points and references so comfortably readable.

Let me touch on a few fundamental notions, as he terms them.

Put together everything known about MAN and we find, first, that he had to "live." To live, required the second step, man's needs or necessities. This informs us that acts preceded thoughts.

Jumping way forward, through the eons, we find that through imitation, repetition, group- and tribal-living, "a way of life" developed. The motives were need and, later, interest and desire. From which come the traits we have often listed, including greed, hope, fear, and so on.

What was produced and remains is "habit in the individual and custom in the group."

When ruminating contrarily, we note habits and customs and check the attitude of the Crowd to see what motives may be swaying people in the wrong direction. By wrong direction, I simply mean the Crowd often goes off at a tangent, which is found later to have been "a bum steer," to use the vernacular. This may be because the Crowd is purposely *led* in a wrong direction or because the groups became emotionally aroused over a given subject.

Instinct and impulse have to do with our studies: the former being an inherent force, the latter commonly arising from imitation and from contagion of ideas.

The notion of togetherness, which we hear talked about a good deal, actually goes back to the "beginning." People have gathered in groups for various reasons, but protection, security and survival (satisfaction of needs) are the principal purposes. "Herd instinct" develops group impulses — which are observed in fads, fashions, speculation, and activities of various forms (riots, political mass-meetings, movements, hippies, etc.).

The power of suggestion is really tremendous and can act upon the Crowd in a most telling manner. It creates impulses and impulsive acts. As Professor Sumner comments, "it requires criticism to resist 'suggestion.' An educated man," he continues, "ought to be beyond the reach of suggestions from advertisements, newspapers, speeches and stories. If he is wise, just when a crowd is filled with enthusiasm and emotion, he will leave it and will go off by himself to form his judgment." And that is what the theory of contrary opinion is all about!

THE NAME OF THE GAME

A very noted book was published in 1904, by John Moody, which may have its counterpart someday when the story of Conglomerates is told. Let me set the period with a reprint from the book. This quotation, exactly as it appeared, is too good to miss as it is the trumpeting expression of a great American era, the period of the "Trusts." The quotation is from John Moody's "The Truth About The Trusts:"

"To stop co-operation of individuals and aggregation of capital would be to arrest the wheels of progress — to stay the march of civilization — to decree immobility of intellect and degradation of humanity. You might as well endeavor to stay the formation of the clouds, the falling of the rains, or the flowing of the streams, as to attempt by any means or in any manner to prevent organization of industry, association of persons, and the aggregation of capital to any extent that the ever-growing trade of the world may demand."

This was called the "Standard Oil view" of the Trust movement. It was written by S.C.T. Dodd, then Solicitor of the Standard Oil Company (prior to its being split up into several highly prosperous "Standards," from Jersey to California).

The Trust era marked an exciting period in American finance, and was to make a President famous for "trust busting." The papers in those days, around the turn of the century and into Teddy Roosevelt's term of office, were constantly harping for and against the "bigness" in business as exemplified by the trusts. Many of those early combines came down the years with lasting success. U.S. Steel was one of the biggest, and of course the Standard Oil Companies.

Among the countless descriptions of Trusts perhaps Mr. Dooley's conception was as good as any: A Trust is "somethin' for an honest, ploddin, uncombined manufacturer to sell out to." At least it is expressive — and brings us down to the present era. The same can be said about any number of companies who have sold out to modern combines, which are called Conglomerates.

What suggested the title of this piece was the heading in the Sunday financial section of the *New York Times* during the era. It read, " 'Find Me A Company' Is the Game's Name."

Find-me-a-company fits the modern *Conglomerate* age neatly. I'm a dictionary user. I found definitions for conglomerate, as follows: gathered in a mass, closely clustered; parts collected from various sources, and so on. It struck me as I ruminated over the definitions that an investor would do well to examine his conglomerates to be sure they had not been haphazardly gathered in a *mess*, as well as in a mass.

Don't take this as a crack against these modern combines, as there are many excellently managed ones; but any mania, regardless of how it may be classified — as to quality of its make-up — is subject to contrary examination. This rule is based on the principle that when anything becomes overpopularized, it is likely also to become overextended — or, as we might say, "over-crowded."

How Conglomerates will fare over the long pull is pretty much a matter of judging them individually Some may be broken up again into smaller components. There may be spin-offs, for more efficient management. When the slide-rule boys and the systems-analysts put their findings through their computers they may come up with almost anything; you never know.

However, probably the sum of the parts of better managed combines (if they become "separated" in the future) will be worth more than the combined whole. Maybe we'll see the Standard Oil experience repeated.

The anti-trust agencies have looked into Conglomerates, as you no doubt have noted in your newspapers. In the Journal of Commerce, March 28, 1968, it was reported that "after several years of lenient treatment of conglomerate mergers, the government lawyers have decided that mergers of large business units are harmful to the competition, even when the companies are in different lines of business."

And so we observe the cycle revolving. Turn back and read the opening quotation. Merger, trust, combine, conglomerate: they're all the name of an old game.

"THE GAME IN WALL STREET"

While having the foregoing name-of-the-game in mind I picked up a little book also written back in the time of the Trust Era. It is titled "The Game in Wall Street," and was written by a stock market adviser by the name of J. Hoyle.

It contains a great deal of common sense for stock traders and others. One chapter is called "Hit or Miss Hints." It could have been written today.

For instance, he writes of three-day moves; of chart formations (yes, they used charts back then, too); and suggests that the extent of moves may be measured by the breadth of the foundation (foundation being what writers now call trading ranges or consolidation areas; this was like the modern count system in point-and-figure charts).

He opens the chapter as we might open any talk on the subject of Contrary Opinions. "Greed and impatience are the causes of most of the losses in Wall Street," the author asserts. Who will argue? A few of the "hints" will be interesting to you and show how the principles of stock-market and investment success have been tested by time. I might add how much the Contrary Theory is indebted to the past.

In a bull market the largest volume of transactions is in the advance. The reactions are marked by smaller volume. The reverse is true during a bear campaign.

The "tips" and "points," and "they say" and "we hear," and the gossip of so-called financial papers, as well as the letters of advertising brokers, ought not to be allowed to influence your views as to the course of the market. (We contrarians go a step farther and check the *opposites.*)

It's the darkest before the dawn . . . Anticipate! Anticipate! Anticipate!

Don't be either a chronic bull or a chronic bear.

A bull campaign may be divided into three periods: 1st Period — A sneaking bull market.

2nd Period — A creeping bull market.

3rd Period — A final grand rush, (with wild-cat and red-dog stocks galloping to the front amid great excitement).

Finally, the author, J. Hoyle, 80 years ago, before the 1920's and the Big Crash, before the New Deal, before the SEC, before The Great Society, and prior to conglomerates, billion-dollar funds, and the new millionaires in Wall Street — finally in his little book he wrote:

"What everyone expects does not happen in Wall Street."

To which we say *Amen* — and be sure to be contrary.

FUNDS FOLLOW THEIR OWN CROWDS

Perhaps you recall an article in the Wall Street Journal, concerning the actions of Funds, in respect to investment timing.

The Ruminator has touched on this thesis every now and then. It is important to recognize that managers of portfolios for institutions, mutual funds and similar large aggregations of capital, tend to act in concert — rather than as individuals.

This became conspicuous in 1968 (a) during the early winter when stock prices faded, (b) again in the way funds accumulated large cash reserves during the January-March quarter, and then (c) in the manner in which they crowded into the market during those record days in the forepart of April. It was as if a leader gave signals and they all responded.

Moreover, no doubt there was crowding to a considerable extent in the same securities. The Marchend reports showed to what extent Mutual Funds held money uninvested. Quarterly reports appear in the Commercial & Financial Chronicle, Wiesenberger's Investment Company Reports, and in other media. The Wiesenberger figures, showed common-stock funds with cash-and-governments from 15 to 25% and more. This is extremely high and accounted for the stupendous volume of purchasing that occurred in April's hectic trading.

What such periods mean to you and me is that not only do we need to observe the Crowd — referring to the public sector of investors and traders — but we must also pay close attention *to what the funds are doing.* Fund managers make up a crowd of their own, including those in major Trust Companies.

Let me add one more thought in this connection. The competition among portfolio managers, to present a striking record at the end of each quarter, has developed the cult of the performance stock. Salesmen for Mutual Funds naturally like to have a "hot" fund to offer, so we witness more and more attention being paid to fast-moving growth stocks than to the more conservative so-called Blue Chips.

The time was to come when the performance stocks toppled off their high-wires for longer than simply a brief period for re-accumulation. But until that time arrived, fund managers were forced by competition to show a record of attractive quarterly capital gains.

It is a case of "the buyer beware." Why shouldn't he, if he demands quick gains? Fast profits require fast footwork, which equals PROPORTIONATE RISKS.

As I have ventured to comment so often, we live in a speculative era. We have to accept it — or ignore it at peril to our pocketbooks.

BE YOUR OWN RUMINATOR

There Are No Think-Tank Franchises

By August, 1968, Wall Street reached the stage in the Great Bull Market of the 1960's when amateur and professional alike benefitted from ruminating over financial pitfalls, among which the franchise, conglomerate, and new issue markets were conspicuous.

With the then current popularity of franchises the Ruminator reminded his readers that there were no franchises available for think-tanks.

You can rent a computer to do your figuring for you, but someone has to think up what to feed the electronic monster.

Notwithstanding the extraordinary success of some franchises — one always spoke of Kentucky Fried Chicken when the subject came up, but there were many older established franchised businesses that have done very well, too — but notwithstanding the successes, the time had come to ponder the point that all good things can be overdone.

In the Wall Street Journal, or in the financial pages of any large metropolitan newspapers, one found numerous advertisements of freshly manufactured stock certificates offered for sale, many for new franchise schemes.

Offerings of new issues are tempting to the stock buyer. They are tempting because any number of these new issues have doubled and tripled in price, almost as soon as released.

Issuing new shares of new companies is a popular activity when a big bull market develops and volume of trading expands. And why not? Everybody wants to get rich quick and what easier way than to buy shares in some new venture that will double overnight? When one reads how well some franchise is doing, he says to himself, "A license to sell Doodle Pads should be a real winner."

Unfortunately, these "quickies" aren't easy to pick up; that is, the good ones. Suppose you note the name of one of the brokers in the underwriting group, in an advertisement in your paper. You call him up. You ask if you can pick up a few shares of the Doodle-Pad Company. His answer will probably be, "Sorry, but the shares have been disposed of."

You shake your head and wonder how come nothing is available. You then look to see later if the shares have been issued and what the price is of Doodle-Pad. When you note the price is twice the offering figure you get hot under the collar, but there's nothing to do about it. You can pay twice the offering figure or forget it.

In some instances it pays to reach and fork over the boosted price, but this much may be said: One doesn't blindly pay double unless he can afford to lose. The record books are full of new issues that fell in price as fast as they rose. An early riser often becomes an after-sinker. This was true of the 1968-1969 new-issue market.

THE ART OF SUCCESSFUL SPECULATION

Everyone Is A Speculator Today

The art of successful speculation consists of think ing in the *future*, and of *thinking contrarily*. To be successful in speculation requires (a) an extraordinary amount of general and specific knowledge, (b) a keen sense of "money" and, perhaps the most important of all, (c) a temperament that thrives on the strains and tension of speculative money-making (and money-losing, be it added!).

Above all, an understanding of the Theory of Contrary Opinion is essential to thinking speculatively.

When you stop to realize how unprepared most people are when they attempt to speculate you marvel they don't lose more money. Professions require postgraduate education before one is qualified to practice — whether it be as a physician, an engineer, a lawyer, or a certified public accountant.

Yet, you find people speculating who cannot read or understand the simplest balance sheet or comprehend the profit-and-loss system. The significance of static versus ladderlike earnings is lost as they grasp eagerly for tips.

May I insert, therefore, a definition, so we'll have a clear understanding?

According to Webster, speculation comes from the Latin, speculare, meaning intuition, vision, perception, the faculty of intellectual examination — and especially, *reasoning* in the form of systematic analysis. To speculate, means to spy out, to observe; hence a speculator is a contemplator and an observer, one who looks ahead intelligently, intuitively, and perceptively.

I stress the definitions because the art of successful speculation means to *cast your mind into the future,* while observing the present. This isn't a catch phrase. Think about it a moment. You can examine the present and get a reaction that everything seems to be running along smoothly. That's that. The speculator examines the present and his reaction is that everything seems to be running in a direction that will lead to a boom, or to a recession; or that conditions suggest changes ahead that are presently unpredictable.

The foregoing emphasis on the necessity for a speculative attitude is justified because under prevailing (and foreseeable) world tensions everything is speculative, even life itself. It follows that everyone is a speculator today.

From a speculative point-of-view, stocks are made to sell. This takes us at once into the future. A money-player concentrates on the future, not on the present. He avoids the stand-still companies and chooses those with future growth.

It is not present or current income that interests the speculator. He is after a capital gain in the future. In sum, successful speculation means analyzing contemplated purchases (whether stocks, commodities or real estate) with one end in view: Shall I be able to sell this holding in the future for more than I paid for it? That demands the second question: Am I buying it at the right time?

Remember the merchant's maxim: Well bought is half sold.

The *timing question*, in turn, entails the employment of contrary checking. A contrary analysis of popular opinions concerning the period, and the speculation one has in mind, plus a survey of what groups of professionals are doing in the same field, will provide information which will unquestionably aid the contrary-minded speculator in *timing* his purchases and sales with consistent success.

The gold standard, as we know it, is relatively a modern monetary system, dating from 1774, in England — about the time of the Industrial Revolution and the American Revolution.

In the United States, however, we operated our personal affairs and commercial undertakings on the bi-metallic standard until the Act of 1853. We were "off gold- from the early Civil War days until January 1, 1879 — the Specie Resumption Act of 1873, put us squarely on the single gold standard, which finally went into effect in January, 1879.

It is helpful to an understanding of the monetary system to recognize that although gold has more desirable qualities, and is more trustworthy as a standard of value, than any other commodity, the facts are that nations have been "going on and off gold" — and devaluating their currencies — with aggravating monotony.

To complete the run-down, the United States abandoned the convertible gold standard, as we know to our regrets, in 1933 — and in 1934 revaluated gold at $35 an ounce (from $20.67). Over 40 countries had suspended gold payments in 1931-32, following Great Britain's devaluation of the pound sterling on September 21, 1931.

Now, a generation later, we find ourselves in a two-price gold era: an official figure of $42.22 an ounce and a fluctuating market price. Again gold is attracting world attention and has become once more a gambling commodity as well as a monetary medium of international trade. As for a store-of-value: first, we Americans can't buy it; and second, its value fluctuates in accordance with demands and supplies from all points of the compass, including South Africa where the big gold mines are located.

While gold is presently gyrating in price as wildly as in the New York gold market of a century ago, nevertheless predictions on the future of gold are at best a random shot.

Anything as sought after as gold is certain to cause pain as well as pleasure. Even a brief reading of the history of currencies makes one realize the temptations of rulers and dictators to depreciate their coinage by various methods such as clipping and alloying.

Incidentally, I wonder where in history one finds a grosser job of alloying than has occurred in our copper sandwiches?"

There have been numerous depreciations of the English shilling and the French sou, and of Italian coins; a contrarian may ponder what the final out- come will be of our mutilated silver coins. Those who were in France in 1918 will recall how the peasants and working people charily counted out their big copper sous when about to purchase bread and wine. It was not long before the sou was worthless as a medium of exchange.

Gold has been a popular speculative vehicle, as well as a monetary medium. Speculation occurs with any commodity that changes in price. In the case of gold, speculation occurs in the commodity that measures the values of other commodities.

The result of gold speculation, in consequence, can cause economic turbulence at times.

Let us go back a hundred years, to the Greenback Era, when gold was traded from morning 'till night, in gold markets and in hotel lobbies.

Because of the demands of the Civil War, gold was abandoned in 1861 and the paper dollar— to be known ever after as "greenbacks" — fast depreciated in value. This was in the north. In the south, the Confederacy commenced printing paper money of various denominations, as they had to have something as a medium of exchange.

The writer has a number of sheets, printed by the Bank of South Carolina, dated Feb. 1, 1863. Each sheet contains 18 small rectangles, 33/4 x 21/2 inches, printed with the currency value of each piece. One cut off the slips, I suppose, before pocketing the money. The full sheet, 12 x 15, has four twenty-five cent slips, eight of seventy-five cents each, and six each for fifty cents: $10 in all.

At the outbreak of the Civil War, in April, 1861, a minor stock-market break in New York was the forerunner of a financial crisis late in the year — which, in turn, resulted in New York banks' suspending specie payments, to stop the drain on their gold. The first issuance of greenbacks occurred in February, 1862— untied to, and unbacked by, gold. Gold was quickly hoarded.

Speculation immediately was rife. As the price of gold was pushed up, the greenbacks lost value — until at the worst, these paper dollars sank to 35¢ relative to gold. And this meant that purchasing power decreased sharply, because of inflated gold prices. It cost the government dearly, in its war expenditures — and everybody felt the pinch, of course.

In October, 1864, the New York Gold Exchange was formed. Speculation increased enormously (evening trading had been active at the old Fifth Avenue Hotel, until banned because the boys were too noisy!). In 1864 a magnificent building was constructed at the corner of Broadway & 24th Street, adjoining the hotel. Called *Gallagher's Evening Exchange,* it enjoyed a nightly attendance of 600, sometimes rising to 1200 when excitement became feverish.

The black day for gold, as readers will recall, was September 24, 1869 — known ever since as Black Friday — when Jay Gould, with the aid of James Fisk, tried to corner gold. Through Washington connections and contact with A. C. Corbin, President Grant's brother-in-law, Gould thought he could prevent the government from selling gold from its reserves. It is pleasant to relate that U.S. Grant saw through the wicked scheme and at the crucial moment, with gold selling at 155, and just touching 160, a wire arrived on the floor of the Exchange reading:

> *The Treasury will sell, at 12 o'clock noon tomorrow, four million gold and buy four million bonds, Proposals will be received in the usual form.*
>
> *Daniel Butterfield,*
> *Assistant Treasurer*

In today's language, that was the end of the ball game. Gould had been sneakily unloading some of his gold, when he began to wonder if the President might not get wise at what he was up to. His confederates, however, were cleaned and several went into bankruptcy. Brokers, too, went bust. The penalties were indeed sad to record: failures, suicides, and ruin.

Thus ends a short account of gold, which we liberty-loving Americans are not permitted to buy — our ownership can only be as shareholders in gold mines.

As gold fluctuates, so do the thoughts of speculators.

WILL EVERYBODY SOON BECOME A CONTRARIAN?

This question is frequently asked: Will everyone, learning about contrary opinions, shortly become a practicing contrarian?

We are safe, I think, in answering in the negative. The quick reply is a cynical one: People as a whole do not think, period. In consequence, they are not suddenly going to commence to think contrarily; or to analyze why this or that condition will fail to work out as predicted, or why a given forecast will be wrong as to its timing.

It is true that more and more security analysts are adopting the *idea* of contrary selections of stocks. That is, an analyst will remark that a given recommendation is attractive because it has temporarily lost its popularity. (It will shortly regain it, he prophesies — which could be wishful-thinking, of course.)

Another analyst, using a more studied contrary approach, will uncover what seems to be sound grounds for expecting increased earnings of a company that will be a surprise to the investment advisory fraternity. When a selection of this character turns out as contrarily theorized, the stock may well have an attractive rise when other analysts see it come to life.

So it is that analysts more and more will adopt the contrary approach. Competition among hundreds of analysts in mutual funds stimulates the hunt for stocks that are neglected, but have brighter prospects than generally recognized. Success depends obviously on the extent of analysts' digging for facts generally unknown or unrecognized, and on their judgement on the market, and in the future.

Here we come to the place where I think you will agree that there never will be too much company on the contrary side. The contrary approach to the various trends that affect and influence stock prices is a separate and distinct study from the individual selection of stocks.

Weighing the opinions of the numerous groups that make up the total Crowd that gives us contrarians an opposite approach to follow is a task in *thinking* that few will bother to undertake.

It is far easier for the average person to accept what he reads in the paper or hears in the locker room about the condition of business, or of some political problem, or of monetary questions, for example, than it is to sit down and ferret out the probabilities from *concentrated contrary thoughtfulness.*

The Theory of Contrary Opinion will never be- come so popular that it destroys its own usefulness. Anything that you have to work hard at and to think hard about, *to make it workable*, is never going to become common practice.

INVESTORS' AGE GAP

The renewed monetary crises — with gold back in the headlines — remind us again of the "age gap" among investors and traders. It is a question contrarians learn to deal with. This is another aspect of the usefulness of the Theory of Contrary Opinion.

You find the age gap especially in these categories of present-day economics:

A. Gold and Technology

B. Depressions

The older investor feels more secure if he has some representation of "gold" in his portfolio. This is because he was brought up under the Gold Standard. He may hold North American gold mining stocks or those of South Africa — or he may hold gold bullion abroad somewhere (this latter is not too common, as we U.S. citizens are not supposed to own gold).

Where the younger investment minds have an advantage — and a distinct one, I wish to emphasize — is in their liking for, and understanding of, what I'll lump under one head as "science stocks." The technological era is far better comprehended by young analysts and economists than by those born prior to World War One. The older minds think more in terms of production efficiency gained from the assembly lines created by Henry Ford that became so advanced during the war years. Guns, trucks, ships and all forms of armaments (and the early airplanes) brought forward a new era in American industrialism. This is what we older folks grew up with. The industrial might of America was as magical back in the epoch starting in 1915 as the technological revolution that has developed in the years since World War II.

Minds are slow to catch up with the realization of new innovations unless prodded continually. A glance at any list of innovations (technical, medical, chemical, and others) reveals the extraordinary discoveries and developments of just the past third of a century: this one generation's creativeness is startling. Going back a full century one finds the list includes countless things we take for granted: the typewriter, the telephone, linotype machine, internal combustion engine, incandescent electric light, X-rays, and on into the years of penicillin, radar, jet engines, nylon, nuclear physics, computers, and so on.

It is no wonder that the average mind has become so crowded with "developments" that the older innovations are retained more sharply than yesterday's discoveries. This suggests that the contrarian must constantly bring his mind up to date if he wishes to be *au courant.*

Speaking of innovations, J. J. Servan-Schrieber, noted author of the fast-selling book, "The American Challenge," points out that *the intellectual* is coming into his own. Every country, every big business, demands IDEAS and INNOVATIONS, in order to control the technological revolution and bring themselves forward in total world affairs.

Turning to the thoughts of depressions, it is the oldsters that tend to compare their opinions of conditions with the great era of the 'Twenties and the crash that followed. This is not a strange phenomenon, actually. I can recall my father referring to the great depression of the 1890's — and the panic of 1893. That was the time of reference for the businessmen and investors of the years after the turn into the 20th Century, and on into the war years. Bonds were the "in thing" in later days. Boys coming out of the Ivy League schools and colleges 50 years ago, and young men coming back from the war, "went into the bond business." The National City Bank of New York had sales offices for bonds in numerous cities. I also recall how bankers went into South America to bring back 7% and 8% bonds to sell to American investors. (A sorry tale, so I'll not enlarge on it!)

The bond-selling era dried up during the 1920's, when the stock-market boom got under way — and the common-stock era, in turn, was buried under the avalanche of the 1929 crash and the ensuing toboggan and depression. For a time — some years, in fact — Wall Street was a most unpopular place. Stock exchange houses had great difficulty obtaining young recruits who wanted to learn the business. Wall Street did not really come back in popular esteem from an employment standpoint until after the second World War. The depression had lasted until 1939, and then the war years of the 1940's were upon us (which brought economic recovery).

What younger contrarians perhaps should pay more attention to, is a study of economics and monetary ramifications in an effort to determine in their own minds whether they, too, will experience a drastic depression as in the past — or if they are satisfied that the "New Economics" will continue to operate without the sharp busts. The last five years give one reason for thought.

We can see from the great upheavals of the past why it took *time* for interests to shift about. And also we can understand why investment-minded people, whose active experiences have been within the past 25 years, have a different outlook from those whose recollections and experiences cover the great swings of this startling 20th Century.

As I Ventured To Write In December, 1968

A consistent effort to gain perspective is essential for the successful investor and speculator in order that he may ride through a future that may be as "swinging" from an economic standpoint as the past decades have been. Indeed, with the build-up of the 1960's now running into its tenth year it behooves us contrarians to be careful and contrary. The ending years in the decades (1969) have commonly been periods of upsets and wind-ups. Stock-marketwise, the "nine years" have been, on the average, difficult ones for both investors and speculators. Look back sometime and note the varying trends as the decades have ended. Cyclically, there is enough evidence to warrant one's being wary in the "nines," especially when the year before has been as excitable as 1968 has been.

The foregoing will be more readily acceptable to older readers, but the younger ones will go along with me, I hope.

Let us all keep our contrary wits about us in 1969, although things are bright at present, in this December of 1968.

I can't close this new-versus-old rumination, without a reminder that our go-go stock market, which we have been enjoying since the fall of 1966, is elevated on stilts that can become wobbly without warning. "A stilt formation in the stock market," as a good friend of mine used to say, "is one to get out from under." Only one stilt has to give way to bring down the whole structure. I suggest this is a caveat to ruminate over between now and New Year's.

MERGERITIS

An Inflamed Game That Cooled Off As Prices Fell

Several pages back (page 31) I wrote about conglomerates, titled *The Name of the Game.* I referred to John Moody's famous 1904 book, *The Truth About The Trusts.* (Names are changed in history: corporate trusts become conglomerates, and investment trusts become mutual funds.) That former era of corporate togetherness made history, as this one will.

It is safe to predict that there will be newsworthy aftermaths to the recent-time merger movement. The trust era at the turn of century made Teddy Roosevelt notorious for his "trust busting" activities and led to the break-up of the Standard Oil Company.

The holding company mania in the 1920's took years to unravel, especially in the utilities. Wheelers and dealers today adopt many of the financial schemes learned in former periods of high-flown speculation.

It is descriptive to name the game mergeritis, as the dictionary tells us the suffix itis means inflammation. Certainly the conglomerate craze has been, and is, inflamed, from the standpoint of speculation.

Since the conglomerate mania, we have seen their prices slide off, some rather sharply. So I feel my contrary-slanted remarks were timely in 1968.

Nevertheless, these combines have — and will have — a big place in American corporate life, so permit me to record another chapter in the story.

Fortune Magazine asserted in its February, 1969, issue that "the great conglomerate movement is generating wide-spread doubt, apprehension and even dismay." It was reminiscent of the robber baron days. Roy Ash of Litton, and G. William Miller of Textron, have both denounced "mergers by the numbers," which *Fortune* interpreted as referring to "combinations in which sound planning for *internal* growth is subordinated to mere piling up of assets."

Heinz Biel, a respected and knowledgeable broker with the experience of having lived in Germany in 1923 where, he says, one paid billions of marks for a postage stamp, was a severe critic of the corporate take-over game. "The take-overs," he said, "result in the printing of money. Corporations, not the government, are printing the lousiest kind of securities — debentures — to pay for take-overs."

(These remarks were recorded at a dinner-table conference of the Center for the Study of Democratic Institutions, at the Harvard Club, early in February, 1969.) It was the rawest kind of inflation Biel feels; it amounts to "options . . . selling for money."

It was a most opportune subject for contrarians to ruminate over, considering the "sorting out" that followed.

MERGER MANIA SOON COOLED OFF

The merger mania was far larger than in previous similar eras. According to W. T. Grimm & Co., of Chicago, a firm that keeps tabs on these activities, there were well over 4,000 deals consummated in 1968, far more than in any other year (around 3,000 in 1967 and under 2,500 in 1966). It was big business indeed, this putting together of big outfits to make bigger ones. When you look at the stock page you see a string of preferred shares and bonds following the quotations of the common shares. All very well, if we never have bad times when it be- comes difficult to pay interest charges and dividends on the preferreds. The conglomeration of these "debt securities" are a worry to officials.

Let me quote conglomerate executive, Mr. L. F. Avnet, who was concerned about the trend of the take-over movement. This is what he said:

> "A demonstration of efficiency in the more customary operating areas, as manufacturing, sales, purchasing and personnel administration may not be enough (in 1969). The mood of shareholders will call for dramatic improvements in the income statement. More importantly, it will also call for constant and significant rise in equity value."The net result will be even greater reliance by management on mergers and acquisitions as a means of achieving the sharply higher profitability and equity values it will take to compete for institutional and individual investor funds."

As you think more and more about the uncertainties facing American business, and dwell on the point in the first sentence above, you realize that business management today differs from management efficiency of only a few, years ago.

What we see all about us is "systems analysis" and "systems efficiency" stressing the factor of (a) technological control in *running* a business, and (b) money-and-merger control in *expanding* a business.

The executive and successful acquisitions' expert whom I quote above added this second sharply pointed remark to his comments: "Mergers and acquisitions, however, represent a new kind of ball game for many managers. The New Year (1969) will see a sharp drop in the number of sound merger situations which are available; it will also see a greater abundance of self-appointed but hazardous or worthless acquisition candidates. . .

The acquisition game was, and is, a conspicuous example of a financial fervor (contagion) that contrarians will observe with vigilance. Acquisitionists are eager-beavers. The striving for profitability can carry them away when a "dear is offered to them. As warned above, the number of questionable mergers that may be consummated from year to year test our ability to sidestep temptation, as speculators, without first being contra-minded evaluators.

Mergeritis — An Inflamed Game: I think you will agree the analogy fits. It has become a subject of concern among Stock Exchange and SEC officials, in the Congress, and in the anti-trust division of the Justice Department. From which good will come.

EVENTS LEAD THE LEADERS

A subject to which we contrarians do not pay sufficient attention is where EVENTS lead the leaders.

Perhaps it would be more descriptive to say "where events *drive* the leaders." By way of illustration, suppose we are watching an exciting television "western." The stage coach is careening down the road, the six-horse team in full gallop, with the hold-up boys in hot pursuit. The frightened leaders, with nostrils pointing and hooves pounding, are fighting the driver who hopes to control the team while giving the leaders their heads.

I don't want my readers to fear the coach went off the road and into a gully, smashing the money trunk and killing a passenger, so let me put you at ease. The cowboy next to the driver swung around and with his trusty six-shooter caught one of the bad guys square in his shooting arm, knocking him off his horse. The other two pulled up (they seem to run in three's, you may have noticed) to help their buddy, while the driver steadied his coach-and-six and went on down the road.

This is a clear illustration, I'm sure you will agree, of an event controlling actions!

In a more modern (yet little more enlightened) era, we find bad guys shooting it out with good guys all over the world.

Whether it be in the dark of night in a slum area (or even in New York's Central Park), or in the jungles of southeast Asia, the fearful practice of *taking lives* has become a CONTROLLING EVENT that is throttling decisions that otherwise would make for normal and peaceful existence.

The Psychology of Revolts and Riots

Much of what is happening in recent times comes under the general head of "psychology of revolts and riots," or as Gustave Le Bon titled it in one of his later books, *The Psychology of Revolution.** Primarily a study of the French Revolution, its findings and principles are applicable to the problems of the era.

> Le Bon steers our contrary ruminations when he asserts that "a great number of historical events are often uncomprehended ... because we seek to interpret them in the light of a logic which in reality has very little influence upon their genesis."

From this, in the light of current events, we can comprehend how it is that events are controlling our daily lives to a degree few recognize, or even are willing to accept. And events obviously are controlling the Administration and the Congress.

We constantly look to Washington to stop this, control that, solve these problems and correct those.

We are ruled by the psychology of crises. "The historians who judged the events of the French Revolution in the name of logic could not comprehend them, since this form of logic did not dictate them." Is it not the same nowadays? Logic would have ended the Vietnam war years sooner. Logic likewise should solve the race ques-

---

*Reprinted in paperback edition by Fraser Publishing Company, Burlington, Vt. Le Bon's "The Crowd" is also in paper-back edition.

tion, one would think. Unfortunately, psychology and emotions are not a part of logic.

Thus it is that events are controlling our decisions, our determinations, and our destinies. And events are too often uncontrollable.

I may add that the reason this is a subject for contrarians follows from this further quotation: "When any question gives rise to violently contradictory opinions we may be sure it belongs in the realm of beliefs and not to that of knowledge." Do we not find violently contradictory opinions in almost every vital question that arises today, including those in the area of finance and socio-economics?

Indecisions Often Arise from Decisive Events

In the vast realm of indecisions the theory of contrary opinion is of tremendous help.

Behind the outbreaks, the riots, the mugging and the weird forms of dissent lie what has become an almost overpowering sense of frustration everywhere. Youths express it in rebelling against authority. We find it in the race problem. Yet, logic does not explain or dictate the actions; nor did it explain the war in the jungles of southeast Asia, and the inability of "men of reason" being able to have earlier resolved the conflict. Perhaps you will say the men on the "other" side were not men of reason, but men of unreasoning hatred of Americans.

Suppose we see what Le Bon has to say about the factor of *hatred.* The book, you remember, is primarily focussed on the French Revolution.

"The hatred of persons, institutions, and things which animated the men of the Revolution is one of these affective phenomena which are the more striking the more one studies their psychology. They detested, not only their enemies, but the members of their own party. . . ."

We can think of similar traits in our time.

The comment goes on to point out how *hatred* is magnified in wars — and I might add, how it expands in periods of dissension.

Human traits, as we know, are the characteristics that make our contrary theory workable and useful. We may include hatred as a most important one, when considering Crowd agitations and revolts of various types. We may be thankful, however, that hatred can and does fade out, frequently as fast as it builds up.

To sum up, events control actions and attitudes of individuals and of Crowds. Contrarians, therefore, look for contrary guidance in the EVENTS as well as in the analysis of viewpoints, sentiment and activities of those concerned.

THE FAIRYLAND OF FINANCE

THE GOOD FAIRIES VISIT WALL STREET

The good fairies have surely been waving their wands generously in Wall Street the past two or three years. Numerous fortunes have blossomed from thin air, as youthful operators waved their wands.*

*(This piece stands as first written in April, 1969.)

It would be more accurate reporting to say the fortunes blossomed from thin capitalizations, rather than from thin air, but the meaning is similar.

Old-timers recall the 1920's and say, "Shucks you haven't seen anything. You ought to have seen the way Mike Meehan ran radio in the old days; that took skill and tactical manipulation. Today's kids don't know what it's all about."

Maybe the young operators don't know what it's all about, from a 1929 viewpoint, but they surely know what it takes to make a million bucks sprout from a bank loan!

There is one immeasurable difference between the pool operators of the old days and the fund operators of today. I have commented on it before, but it bears repeating as it is the nub of this whole question of market manipulation (if I may still use this descriptive, but naughty word).

Those who are running stocks today — that is, are managing what are known as performance funds — are operating on other people's money. They do not have a clique of well-heeled speculators breathing down their necks, watching to see if their man will be able to unload the long line of stock he accumulated without breaking the market and losing all the profits.

About the worst pressure on the average portfolio manager today is the three-month date-line that lies before him when he has to show publicly what he has been doing. He doesn't have hardshelled speculators telling him to get going and "push that stock up."

Another significant dissimilarity has become more evident in recent months.

Above I referred to "thin capitalizations" which have afforded happy hunting in the Wall Street fairyland. In the former era of speculative frenzies, the pool managers avoided the stocks with small number of shares outstanding; they needed the companies with big capitalizations in order to attract a large public following when their stocks became active. The only way to get the public to follow them was to "advertise" the stock on the tape. That is, to keep it moving, both up and down, but with the price pointing upward.

You can accumulate the shares in a thinly capitalized company, too, of course. However, as you do it you will advance the price without having time to gain a public following. Actually, the performance managers prefer not to pick up an outside following. The shares will remain in the fund until a time comes when they can be gradually liquidated, or perhaps until a time when a "secondary" (or "block") *distribution* can be arranged. The point is that the distribution of the shares is not the all important factor in today's performance game. In former times, the game wasn't finished until distribution had been completed. Today, *without the distribution* the fund's asset value (and advertised price) shows an increase — as the various stocks move up under heavy buying. The fund gains from the advertised asset value that reflects smart portfolio handling, *thereby obtaining the following that really counts: shareholders in the fund.*

This fairyland of finance is all flowers and sunshine so long as nothing happens to upset the stock market other than the so-called intermediate declines we have experienced in recent years — e.g. 1968 and 1966, or even the more extended drop in 1962. These setbacks do not last long enough to discourage investors, besides which investors are more and more becoming fund-minded. Until something drastic occurs, the public is likely to believe that "the funds can do no wrong.- (The "something drastic" did develop later in 1969 and in 1970.)

As I write, however, a "mutual fund investment index" published in *Barron's*, shows that things don't always go just the way the fund operators have in mind. For 1969, up to March 27, the managed portfolios in all mutual funds reported on by the Arthur Lipper Corporation failed to do as well as the "unmanaged" mathematical market indexes, including the Dow Jones Industrials, Standard & Poor's, and the New York Stock Exchange composite average. Interestingly enough, the poorest performance in those 12 weeks was in the 217 "growth-stock" funds.

The foregoing is important, if only to note for contrarians that everything cannot be taken for granted in Wall Street's fairyland, even mutual funds. It is not to say that mutual funds are not excellent investments. The majority of them are, no doubt, but that doesn't mean the portfolio managers will catch every wiggle in the stock market, or will always "beat the averages." The measurement of excellence must be the long pull, not just a few weeks, or months.

A Radio Pool of 1928

I mentioned the name of Mike Meehan earlier in this piece. Readers might like to have a quick review of one of Mr. Meehan's shortrun radio plays. This one happened back in 1928. Radio was indeed the good fairy of those wonderful days of reckless speculation, when everyone knew there was pie in the sky if he only got aboard the right stock to ride up there.

I'll take my review from Barnie F. Winkelman's entertaining and illustrated book, *Ten Years of Wall Street* (John

C. Winston Co., 1932). I recall the days myself but the facts and figures come from the book.

A preamble to Mr. Winkelman's book is worth reprinting:

On the following pages we have set forth the series of events by which a public, that in 1921 had forsworn stock speculation, was brought back into the market in 1928 in greater numbers than ever before.

One can shift the dates with equal meaning, to 1968.

The "pyrotechnics in Radio . . . had been engineered by a syndicate of some sixty-three participants," the author tells us. The names he included were the most familiar speculators of those times: Brady, Raskob, Percy Rockefeller, Durant, Chrysler, Swope, Fisher Brothers, and others. "The presiding genius of the pool was Michael J. Meehan, the Radio specialist on the Floor (of the New York Stock Exchange)."

The day before the pool started operations, Radio was selling at $74 a share. Soon, after Mr. Meehan got busy, it reached $109.25, as tremendous activity picked up. "The tremendous activity brought the public into the market."

To brief the story, Mr. Winkelman reports that "the pool represented an investment of 13 million dollars, and in this short period (of actually only a few days) its profits totalled five million or 39 percent. The price dropped to 101 immediately after the pool ended its activities, and five days later was back to 87."

Numerous pool operations lasted longer, of course, and many were unsuccessful. However, millions in profits were taken out of the stock market in those days, as millions are being earned from speculative operations in these days. Space in this reprint edition doesn't permit other recitations, but readers will find the stories of the pools in the Wall Street fairyland of the 1920's excellent mind feeders for contrary thinking.

One thing one learns is that we never quite reach the pie-in-the-sky before the sky clouds over and the deluge comes.

ADVENTURES IN 1969

We can't very well leave the Fairyland of Wall Street without a reference to at least one recent pooling of brains. It was reported in TIME on March 14, 1969.

It seems that staid Standard & Poor's felt they, too, should modernize their advisory division, to become more *performance* in nature. Accordingly, a group headed by Fred Stein (who arrived in Wall Street only a dozen years ago) formed "InterCapital." You might call it a consortium of affluent young millionaires, who have demonstrated they know the secret of the "fast buck." Together with S & P's renamed service they will offer other affluent speculators the opportunity to join them in making their "money multiply," as TIME expressed it. (It occurs to me as I put these pieces into book form, in the winter of 1974, I do not know whatever happened to "InterCapital." I must find out.)

OPINION-FORMING

Events and Opinions Closely Allied

A few pages back we talked about events that so often control the actions of leaders and of crowds.

Let us now discuss how "the people" are controlled, or governed (to use a more democratic word), by an aroused public opinion. (I use *arouse* in the dictionary sense of "to stir to action, to put in motion, to stimulate.")

To keep our ruminations in line, we must again inject the Law of Imitation, which this writer has previously referred to: Gabriel Tarde* explains how the majority imitates the minority. It is interesting in light of the extraordinary student revolts we have experienced, to note this comment of the author:"Every positive affirmation, at the same time that it attracts to itself mediocre and sheeplike minds, arouses somewhere or other in a brain that is naturally rebellious . . . a negation that is diametrically opposite and of about equal strength."

I venture to iterate the assertion "of about equal strength," in that in the greatest number of "imitations" — such as in fashions, games, fads, stocks, and other *manias* — the followers far outnumber the leaders. I agree that the "negation" aroused in some rebellious brain may be of about equal *strength*, but not the *sum* of the brains. In uprisings, the rebellious brains of the leaders are rela-

---

* Paper-back edition of Gabriel Tarde's exceptional treatise, *Tarde's Laws of Imitation*, is available.

tively few, while the sheep-like crowds wave banners, carry signs and trail after the leaders.

Getting back to how people are governed by an aroused public opinion, it is necessary again to note that "an aroused public opinion" does not mean all the people, or all the voters. As Abram Lipsky* reminds us, "when the opinion of the majority is referred to, it is not the numerical but the effective majority that is meant." Yet, merely to say "an effective majority," can be misleading, so I accept the Lipsky definition that "usually Public Opinion means just a vague and unmeasured impression of prevalent opinion."

We contrarians are confronted with the same puzzlement: that contrary opinions are likewise somewhat vague and unmeasurable (except in those cases where polls or votes are taken, and even then a good many are merely "going along" with others of similar views).

> "If left to itself," writes Mr. Lipsky, "public opinion may grow by the slow secular process of trial and error. . . . But public opinion is not left to itself. . . . Persuasion is part of the art of government. It is the business of leaders and statesmen to form public opinion, to direct the thought of a nation in predetermined ways."

Linking the events-controlling and opinion-forming forces together one sees at once how penetrating a contrarian must be in his thinking in order to recognize *where and to what extent he should be contrary-minded.*

First, we have the event; then we have the opinion which the "leader" wishes to implant in our consciousness. It may

---

* In *Man The Puppet, The Art of Controlling Minds,* by Abram Lipsky (Frank-Maurice, Inc. N.Y. 1925).

be a blow-up in a far-off land or a blow-up in Wall Street. We have to analyze the events and then try to judge the possible *contrary* consequences of the happenings, including the influence of the opinion-former.

A crowd-mind is manipulated. A sense of *contact* (physical or mental) is created, by the opinion former. What is sought is the willingness of the crowd, or the masses, to obey a common impulse.

What we contrarians seek is an understanding and interpretation of the crowd-mind. These discussions are an aid in that direction, I hope.

TO KEEP FROM GUESSING WRONG

As we become acquainted with the theory of crowd manipulation, we can "feel":

a how crowds think and act,

b. how leaders (the opinion-formers) think and act,

a. and then how contrarians should think and act.

When we get through these three stages, we also get closer to the solution of *How To Keep From Guessing Wrong*. There is no doubt that "being contrary," as we read or hear general assertions and comments, does prevent thoughtless guessing.

The point is that one cannot turn up a contrary opinion without having *thought about it*. Having thought about it, you cannot very well be *thoughtless*. Q.E.D.!

Events and developments of significance attract attention as they reach a crescendo. This may be illustrated variously.

When a riot occurs, for example, it will attract national attention and the television cameras when it escalates into a mob demonstration of several hundred. If only a dozen or so start a ruckus and fail to gain a following, it is quickly squelched and we never hear about it.

In the stock market, as we all know, activity is what attracts attention and interest. When volume climbs and the tape is late there is an immediate response among traders who want to know what's going on.

The public, too, is attracted more by *activity* than by *price.* Who hasn't heard stories of orders placed when the buyers cared neither for price nor for knowledge of the company. The stock was moving up, the man said: that's all the buyer wanted to know.

It is helpful to remember that when unusual activity is evident in some particular event, *wrong opinions* may be commonplace because of the emotional reactions.

It pays to be contrary when excitement prevails.

MORE ON THE WALL STREET FAIRYLAND

Many years ago, when I first became interested in crowd psychology as it pertained to economics and the stock market, I was fascinated by the famous manias of history, including John Law's Mississippi Scheme, in France; The South Sea Bubble, in England; The Tulip Mania in Holland; The Crusades; and others. (See Charles Mackay's *Extraordinary Popular Delusions and the Madness of Crowds;* it's fascinating reading.)

I recall more than once having mentioned in some writing of mine that among the hundred or more "bubbles" that were foisted on a gullible English public, at the time of the South Sea financing fiasco in 1720, that the prospectus of one of them read, "A company for carrying on an undertaking of great advantage, but nobody to know what it is." (Subscriptions flowed in and the promoter grabbed the money and fled across the channel to obscurity; was never heard from again.)

Naturally, I never expected to see anything like that in *this* enlightened country. (I was about to add "and in this age," when I realized that this age does not appear to be very enlightened, does it?)

Well, let's see. I received a tear sheet from *Forbes Magazine,* of May 1, 1969, that should cap the climax of this bubble story. It is entitled "Success Story." The chronology was presented without comment. We cannot take space for copying in full, but it seems a young man of 22 left graduate school in August 1965 to learn the Wall Street trade of making fast bucks. Switching jobs to gain varying financial experiences, he was ready apparently by December, 1968, to set up his own company, named Integrated Resources, Inc. *Forbes* reports "the assets were $270,000 cash, contributed by his father and a small group of associates. Business: Nil."

In February, 1969, I'm darned if Integrated Resources didn't "go public!" The set-up was 200,000 shares offered at $15 each. The public stock-holders who put up $3 million owned 23%, while the original group owned 77% of the company, and the underwriters received 20,000 shares of restricted stock at 10 cents a share.

But you haven't heard all.

In April, 1969, Integrated Resources traded over-the-counter at $45 per share! Youthful Selig A. Zises, who left graduate school less than four years previously — but who obviously learned the ways of Wall Street fast — had "a paper capital gain," according to the story in *Forbes*, "of 45,000% in about four months."

To conclude: "As of mid-April, the corporate picture was this: Integrated Resources' total market value was $31 million. Assets: $3 million, all cash. Business activities: Pending. End of Story."

CONTRARY OPINION, THE INDIRECT APPROACH TO STRATEGY

The Theory of Contrary Opinion lends itself to a successful *strategy in thinking*. Just as strategy and tactics are the thinking force in warfare, so are they in successful undertakings in industry and finance.

Whereas it is said that warfare is based upon deception, one likes to think that business is conducted, not on deception, but upon competitive strategy.

* Liddell Hart has been called "the captain to whom generals listen;" a former adviser to the British Cabinet General Patton among numerous other admirers asserted "Hart's books have nourished me for twenty years." This book, in paperback, was published by Frederick A. Praeger, in 1954 and has been reprinted several times. Numerous books on military affairs and theory were written by Liddell Hart. (Mr. Hart's original study of "the strategy of indirect approach" was first published in 1929, under the title of *The Decisive Wars of History*.)

Let me turn to the authoritative book on *Strategy*, by B. H. Liddell Hart.* This quotation from the preface of *Strategy* gives a clear conception of what I refer to:

> "When, in the course of studying a long series of military campaigns, I first came to perceive the superiority of the indirect over the direct approach, I was looking merely for light upon strategy.
>
> "With deepened reflection, however, I began to realize that the indirect approach had a much wider application — that it was *a law of life in all spheres: a truth of philosophy.*" (Italics mine.)

Liddell Hart explains this further by saying that the practical achievement of the indirect approach comes when dealing with problems "where the human factor predominates."

Readers readily gather from these references how the more one investigates the advantages of contrary thinking the more important it becomes as a way of arriving at sound viewpoints and profitable strategy.

In war, according to the principles of strategy and tactics, a general endeavors to strike the enemy where and when least expected. He wishes to be sure of the enemy's "unreadiness" for a fight. In the stock market, a big operator's strategy is to swing his line of stocks, either short or long, when he judges the market is least able to "compete" with him; that is, he times his buying when others are selling, and plans his selling when others are ready to buy.

Lesser speculators, as you and I, by adopting the contrary theory can frequently be in league with the Pro and gain the advantages of his strategic plays. Expressed another way, if the purchases and sales we make are opposed to the actions of the "crowd," it is a fair surmise that we are *with* the Pros and contrary to the amateurs.

This again brings up the sensitive point of where fund managers stand in any study of market strategy.

Growth of Funds

From this writer's observations over the past few years, since the growth of new funds has been so prolific, it is evident that we have to calculate in our "indirect approach" on two sets of Crowds, aside from the relatively small number of individual professional traders: one, made up of the public or amateur investors (whose actions are fairly well indicated in the odd-lot transactions that Garfied Drew interprets so effectively); and two, the large and growing group of managers of mutual funds. There, is, also, another professional clique that manages pension funds, and trust funds, but these gentlemen I may characterize as being more investment-minded than the speculative operators of mutual funds. (Mutual funds today are forced, as a practical matter of continuing distribution, to buy and sell shares in what admittedly is a speculative program. The mutual-fund investor (?) demands *action*; the operators endeavor to give him what he wants, knowing he'll redeem his shares and go elsewhere if he doesn't get the action he seeks.)

In sum, we have three groups that enter into what I'll term "the contrary spectrum of strategy:" (a) the public and amateur participants in stock-market trading; (b) operators of mutual funds; and (c) the professional speculators (including specialists, floor traders and big-block negotiators).

The remaining large number, in terms of aggregate purchases and sales of stocks, I place in the category of stock-market stabilizers. They comprise the daily business always being done in securities for purposes other than for short- and long-term profits; estates being settled, trust funds being established or distributed, pension-fund investments, and the multitude of continuing purchases and sales. The total in dollars is huge.

Having these groups in mind, with which one competes when he enters the stock market, let me call on Liddell Hart again for illustrations of strategy that can be made applicable to business and finance.

> "A deeper truth to which Foch and other disciples of Clausewitz did not penetrate fully is that in war every problem, and every principle, is a duality. Like a coin, it has two faces. . . war is a two-party affair, so imposing the need that while hitting one must guard. Its corrollary is that, in order to hit with effect, the enemy must be taken off his guard. . . .
>
> "A further consequence of the two-party condition is that to ensure reaching an objective one should have *alternative objectives.*"

A marginal note in the book before me (written some years ago), reads: In the market, while playing for a rise, one must guard against being wrong. More than that, in considering today's crowded "spectrum," one must continually have before him (when playing the market) the sharp-witted competition he's up against. To move when the opposition is off guard, one must be contrary-minded and constantly on the lookout for "alternative objectives." Contrawise, to move *with* the funds, or the Pros, when that is the evident strategy to follow, requires keen judgment of the "alternatives."

During the latter months of 1969, when one observed the conspicuous reverses suffered by the majority of fund-managers (a decline in average values exceeding the percentage decrease in the Dow Jones industrial average), the value of Contrary Strategy was certainly apparent. In retrospect, the alternative to following the crowd (of fund managers) early in the year was to adopt the tactic of more cash than shares, which was in line with our discussions of the dangerous escalation in speculation.

A final word of counsel from Liddell Hart: "To be practical, any plan must take account of the enemy's (the market's) power to frustrate it."

THINK CONTRARILY YOURSELF

A Do-It-Yourself Recommendation

You will be interested in this reminder, I am sure.

It has become such a common habit to accept what one reads that I wish to urge a do-it-yourself program on all readers of these ruminations.

You will notice at meetings and in seminars that the audience is prone to think alike. This happens especially in meetings where people congregate voluntarily. They are of similar minds or they would not be there. Thus, there may be little contrathinking in the crowd — and usually a general (frequently somewhat sleepy) approval of the comments is voiced.

I have found a similar acceptance among those who show enthusiasm for the theory of contrary opinion. Too many contrarians wish to have the contrary thoughts spelled out for them. The preachment, if I may add it, is this: Think for yourself, too.

Admittedly, everyone has not the time to take all popular questions and sit down to ferret out the contrary angles. However, when it comes to questions close to your pocketbook, or to your personal interest, I believe you will discover many valuable ideas that would otherwise not occur to you if you will dig in yourself to find opposite views or probabilities. Look for the "alternatives."

Although I have been writing on this general subject of contraryism for over 40 years, I repeatedly find myself saying, "Golly, I never thought of that angle," or "How did I overlook *that* contrary viewpoint?"

What it comes down to is that the theory of contrary thinking is more than merely a game to play as if on afternoon television. It is a valuable tool that puts money in your pocket and even affords a more contented manner of living. You don't get all stewed up over every political wisecrack; you realize that "alternatives" do exist.

Beginning contrarians often overlook the temperamental factors involved in the question under study. People continually act from the heart instead of from the brain. Emotionalism dictates actions. One recognizes from this why it is that contrary brain-work can avoid heart-aches from wrong decisions. (It saved heart-aches during "Watergate.")

So — permit this Ruminator to preach the gospel of: *think contrarily for yourself.*

MONEY AND THE CONTRARIAN

This was written (October, 1969) as the experts debated in Washington over high-sounding, highly complex, subjects associated with the International Monetary Fund. The paper-substitute for gold, the SDRs, were accepted. (And now losing status.)

What was so frustrating for the ordinary mortal, be he contrary-minded or crowd-minded, was the fact that the economics of money and credit is the least understood, yet the most influential, of all economic factors. We were to enter a new era of experimentation.

When I look around my library and see the numerous books having to do with money I wonder why it is we know so little about it.

Somehow, when I turn to Brooks Adams (of the famed family that gave us two Presidents and many brilliant descendants), and his noted book, *The Law of Civilization and Decay* (1897), I lose a little of the hopelessness one feels when confronted with monetary and other crises.

Brooks Adams was a peculiarly perceptive student of history. In all his studies and writings he focussed on ideas that are of concern to us who use contrary thinking to aid our understanding.

For example, in the preface to the book, we find this paragraph:

> "Another conviction forced upon my mind, by the examination of long periods of history, was the exceedingly small part played by conscious thought in moulding the fate of men. At the moment of ac-

tion the human being almost invariably obeys an instinct, like an animal; only after action has ceased does he reflect."

I have often mentioned Lincoln's remark that events had controlled him; he hadn't controlled events. One sees the world torn today by uncontrollable events. Decisions are constantly made by-guess-and-by-god, as the old expression has it. Brooks Adams put it this way: "These controlling instincts (in history) are involuntary, and divide men into species distinct enough to cause opposite effects under identical conditions."

Among the "controlling" traits that are especially observed in our practice of contrary ruminating, are Fear and Greed. These two emotional traits come to the surface whenever some monetary event breaks in the news. First we fear what the event will do, and then we try to figure a way to gain by it.

Adams contended that *fear* stimulates the imagination, while *greed* dissipates energy. His thesis is a bit involved, but you get the sense of it, as he suggests that "the velocity of the social movement of any community is proportionate to its energy and mass, and its centralization is proportionate to its velocity; therefore, as human movement is accelerated, societies centralize." Then as they centralize *greed* takes over, so to speak, and the "accumulated capital" theretofore gained becomes the controlling force.

During these stages, monetary "experiments" are continually brought forward. In the autumn of 1969 the latest monetary invention — the SDRs — were being sold to the western world as the great blessing that will free everyone from the "tyranny of gold."

Perhaps the only reliable contrary thought one dares hold when monetary innovations are presented is simply one of *doubt.* Old-timers have confidence only in gold, whereas the younger and "newer" economists are unafraid to experiment with substitutes for what has been called our "barbaric metal." A speaker contends that gold may be barbaric, "but it is no relic."

A review of depressions reveals how in every cycle the crisis developed when money and credit became overextended. No answer to the monetary riddle is foreseeable so long as bankers, businessmen and speculators act *normally*, which is that they will push for profits when, and as long as, there is capital gain to be made. They will leave the idealistic "distaste" for money and the power of money to the hippies.

The trained contrarian recognizes the periods of monetary *over-extension* and guards against the inevitable "corrections." He need not *understand* the riddle of money to avoid its perils.

FUNDAMENTAL NOTIONS OF SOCIOLOGY

"ETHNOCENTRISM"

In my perusals of William Graham Sumner's Folkways, I recently came across a difficult-to-pronounce word that is the technical name for the placard-carriers, anti-anything crowds and dissenters that have attracted so much attention.*

Ethnocentrism is defined as the view or opinion of things and events in which one's own group is the center of everything.

"Each group nourishes its own pride and vanity, boasts itself superior, exalts its own divinities, and looks with contempt on outsiders.

"Each group thinks its folkways the only right ones. . . . Opprobrious epithets are derived from these differences. 'Pig eater,''cow-eater,' `uncircumcised,''jabberers,' are epithets of contempt and abomination."

The name-calling of the police at the Chicago convention in 1968 was an example of Sumner's explanations, as are the epithets we see displayed on cards by the dissenters that parade about today.

Because of the "laws" of imitation and contagion — greatly abetted by seductive, anti-this-and-that emotions —what started out as a *hippie movement* has snowballed into very large groups that make their presence felt, whether at folk-rock festivals (as in Newport and Woodstock, N.Y.) or on the Boston common.

In accordance with Sumner's thesis, this growing number of dissenters has become a large and strongly ethnocentric group.

It is helpful if we, as contrary-minded ruminators, think back and recall times when Americans held strong anti-views against various groups — but which thankfully grew dim with time and finally passed from popular opinion.

In the early days of this century intense feelings were aroused over the "yellow peril," an opprobrious reference

---

* Folkways is issued in a modern paperback edition, at $2.75, and no doubt is available at your bookstore.

to the Chinese. The newspapers that stirred up the sentiments were soon condemned for their "yellow journalism" — a term that persisted for years for sensationalism in the press. The Roosevelt-Hay *Open Door Policy* for China finally dispelled this anti-Chinese prejudice — yet we found ourselves in the second half of the century again extremely concerned, this time over the vast communistic population on the mainland of China which Mr. Nixon finally remedied.

Boston was the center of the anti-Irish rantings in the old days. Many street brawls and broken heads made news that compared in drama with the television sensationalism we cannot escape today when we turn the knob for the evening news.

Even now, a century and more after the war that freed the slaves, and *kept the Union together*, "racism" is an epithet that is hurled about in careless and unjust abandon. The word is used often as a term of hatred toward those against whom the antiestablishment groups hold grudges.

The purpose in this review of fundamental notions in sociology is to stress the thought that in order to understand today's dissident groups we contrarians may fall back upon *perspectives* that demonstrate the accuracy of the saying, "this, too, will pass."

Of course, we have to decide in our own minds whether (1) those of us who disagree with the dissenters, or (2) the dissenters, are the ones who are thinking straight.

Before leaving this subject, Sumner reminds us of two sub-notions of ethnocentrism that bear on the devisive social pattern we are presently in the midst of.

These subsidiary notions are (a) *patriotism* and (b) *chauvinism*, a word which we'll get to in a moment.

Of direct contrary interest is the following quotation from *Folkways*; it is to be noted that Sumner was writing in the closing years of the nineteenth century:

> "For the modern man patriotism has been one of the first of duties and one of the noblest of sentiments. It is what he owes to the state for what the state has done for him, and the state is, for the modern man, a cluster of civic institutions from which he draws security and conditions of welfare. . . ."

Let us see if the word *chauvinism* is any help to us in attempting to find out what has happened to those goose pimples we once felt when we celebrated the Fourth of July with firecrackers and bonfires — and listened to Independence Day speeches. (Old John Adams, you recall, wrote his wife upon the signing of the Declaration that he hoped the day would be celebrated throughout future years in patriotic gatherings, bonfires, and speeches.)

> Sumner remarks that biased feelings "may generate into a vice, as is shown by the invention of a name for the vice: chauvinism. It is a name for boastful group self-assertion. It overrules personal judgment and character, and puts the whole group at the mercy of the clique which is ruling at the moment. It produces the dominance of watch-words and phrases which take the place of reason and conscience in determining conduct. . . ."

Those in the dissident groups can, admittedly, twist the above paragraph around and aim it at their adversaries in the nation-wide controversies over politics, welfare, urban, ethnic or environmental problems — as well as disputes over drugs and morals. To me, it throws light on a national dilemma.

Nevertheless, those of us who endeavor to apply contrary thinking to our daily ruminations find *much* to ruminate over in the fundamental notions of sociology William Graham Sumner writes about so understandingly and entertainingly. Now that this classic is in paperback, thousands of readers become better acquainted with this Yale Professor who was so popular at the turn of the century, a prolific lecturer, essayist and author. Included are many references *to the forgotten man.* Professor Sumner was concerned for the vast middle-class American conservatives — who are still forgotten, but may be on the way back to their rightful recognition.

WE HAVE TO HUNT FOR THE GOOD NEWS

Bad News Is Served To Us

In the opening paragraph of a new book that I find fascinating reading about newspaperdom,* we're told that to journalists ". . . gloom is their game, the spectacle their passion, normality their nemesis."

This is an interesting observation of the notion I have often harped on that contrarians have to go outside the primary news-stories if they wish to find out what is actually going on — and wish to determine what influences

**The Kingdom and the Power,* by Gay Talese, The World Publishing Company, 1969, 550 pages, $10.

may be affecting the trends or problems they are ruminating over.

The bad news is always served to us, hot from the source. *Sensationalism makes news: serenity is boring.* As Gay Talese, the author above quoted writes, "the spectacle" is the passion of newsmen. He went further, which I'll quote, as it, too, applies to contraryism:

> "Journalists travel in packs with transferable tension and they can only guess to what extent their presence in large numbers ignites an incident, turns people on. Press conferences and cameras and microphones have become such an integral part of the happenings of our time that nobody knows whether people make news or news makes people. . . .

Gay Talese's book is about the New York Times, the sub-title telling us it is a "story of the men who influence the institution that influences the world." When you stop to think that the *Times* literally blankets the globe and penetrates "the homes of the mighty," we accept its wide-flung readership as a demand to read it (even if many of us might wish it slanted a bit more to the *right*).

> As of the summer of 1966, the Times was read in 11,464 cities and towns around the nation, in all capitals of the world — 50 copies going to the White House, 39 to Moscow, and even a few sneaking into Peking. News bureaus are scattered everywhere, and the reportorial staff reached from Wall Street to the war-torn jungles of Vietnam. I have been told it has more men covering Wall Street than the Wall Street Journal, but this may be one of those cocktail-party cracks that goes the rounds.

Let me recall the remarks of my late friend, Bob Crawford, that "we only think we think," when we depend upon newspapers, magazines, bulletins, etc., for our information, and fail to go behind the headings, as it were. Now note what Talese says: "News, if unreported, has no impact. . . ." But when reported, we feel its furious impact every day, in newspapers and over the air.

Our contrary task when these sudden news-events happen is to immediately ask ourselves: "What is the possible counter reaction to this unexpected piece of news?"

The great value in reading books like *The Kingdom and the Power* is that they give us a close-up view of what goes on *behind* the news-makers and shows us how they make the news. We have brought home to us what the title suggests, the vast power of the press and the other news media. Television today has become almost over-powering in its ability to arouse emotions, and stimulate crowd reactions. Contagion and imitation have prolific partners in these times of high intensity news. Contrary ruminating — contrary calmness, if I may call it that — can help us avoid being susceptible to the emotional pressures of the press.

Let us never overlook, however, what I quoted at the beginning, that to journalists (whether by print or by air) "gloom is their game, the spectacle their passion, normality their nemesis." So it is that we find it difficult to uncover the normal. It is overshadowed by the spectacular, by the exciting, by the dangerous, by the tragic. The quiet successes are buried on page 39 or 69, or what-not, perhaps alongside the obituaries.

THE WEIGHT OF PREDICTIONS OFTEN THE CAUSE OF THEIR DOWNFALL

In this writer's outline of principles in his *Art of Contrary Thinking*, he ventured a number of sloganized expressions, as is his wont. Pithy remarks put one's ideas over better than wordy explanations sometimes.

One of the principles to follow, in adopting the study of contrary opinions, is to check popular predictions and forecasts. I expressed it as a warning not to be carried away with "what everybody else may be looking at."

> Too many predictions spoil the forecasts; or to put it another way, the weight of predictions often causes their downfall.

What frequently happens, as you have no doubt witnessed, is that a repetition of a given prediction — especially if it comes from an authoritative source — is soon accepted as a belief.

Then what follows is that counteracting policies often are adopted to offset or by-pass the predicted happening, development, or economic event.

For instance, an industrialist who accepts a forecast that a slump will develop six months ahead will cut back well ahead of the time predicted. Thus his action (joined in by other industries) is likely to accomplish one or both results: (1) The slump will come earlier than forecast, and (2) it may well be less serious than anticipated because overextended conditions were corrected earlier.

Then, too, predictions may be *over* counteracted and bring about worse results than forecast. I think the recent dilemma among the money managers is a good example of trying to guess the outcome of forecasts. Many economists believe the danger of "overkill," as they term it, could be as serious as is the danger of a run-away inflation-boom if it is not curbed by tight money.

A considerable amount of research has been done on this question, of the weight of predictions being the cause of their downfall, although it has been limited, I think, to the professional journals. There were brief critical comments in the *Journal of the American Economic Association*, for September, 1963. Comments were on the subject mentioned below, which had been initiated by M. C. Kemp, Professor of Economics at the University of New South Wales, Sydney, Australia. Professor Kemp's thesis appeared in the *American Economic Review*, of June 1962.

> Professor Kemp's article was titled "Economic Forecasting When the Subject of the Forecast is Influenced by the Forecast." He discussed the question of "self-validation of forecasts when the subject is influenced by the forecasts themselves."

The critics got out their slide rules and prepared equations which were soon over my head, as I have neglected my mathematics in the past 50 years. As I have always said, in my work I am concerned with the human figures (what the Crowd does, or is likely to do) and not with the mathematical figures.

The economists finally arrive at a conclusion that forecasts can, and do, influence results, although they bring in numerous ifs and ands to fill their papers. Professor Kemp, in turn, rebuts the critics and asserts, "I can report that the two main conclusions of the earlier papers emerge unscathed: the announcement of point forecasts may be either self-validating or self-destructive; the announcement of direction-of-change forecasts can never be self—destructive." Readers may dig further as they desire. References and bibliography will be found in the September, 1963, *Journal* mentioned.

GUIDANCE FROM THE CROWD

Profit From Their Overdoing and Underdoing

The theory of contrary opinion aims at avoiding Crowd opinions. This is a broad generality, but let it stand for the moment.

The reason for avoiding the crowd in most matters is that the crowd is often wrong. A crowd is swayed by emotion and fear rather than by ruminating and reasoning.

How may we gain guidance from the actions of the crowd? The quick reply might be that if the crowd is usually wrong then if we go contrary to the crowd we shall probably be right.

To an extent this is true, but it is subject to the penalties of being wrong in *timing*. That is, we may be right at the wrong time.

What I am after in this discussion is how we may gain guidance (a) from what the crowd is actively doing, or is thinking about doing; and (b) *what the crowd is not doing.*

THE OVERDOING OF THE CROWD

Let us first take the *overdoing of the crowd.* There are two examples we might use.

I'll refer to investments and speculations, because the crowd's thoughts and actions in the stock market are especially attuned to the contrary theory.

When the crowd goes overboard in its enthusiasm for a given speculation, it is always prudent to analyze thoughtfully what is going on in order to make a judgment" on whether to stay along with the crowd or to leave before the party is over.

When we think of crowds in this respect, let me remind you that we must include the crowd of portfolio managers who today have such vast power in the market, both when they buy in concert (as they seem often to do) and when they dump shares overboard in a sudden decision to desert a position.

Going back to discussions on prior pages, we talked about the franchise craze and although it looked rosy indeed, how it had become a proper subject for cautionary ruminating by contrarians. For illustration and amusement, I picked out Mackay's story in "The South Sea Bubble" about Puckle's Machine Company. This was back around 1711, but promoters had smart ideas in those days, too. Puckle's machine was to revolutionize the art of war, with a new cannon. A versifier described it in this manner (to repeat):

"A rare invention to destroy the crowd
Of fools at home instead of fools abroad,
Fear not, my friends, this terrible machine,
They're only wounded who have shares therein."

You will forgive me for repeating it. I was tempted, in view of what has happened to franchise outfits in recent years. Many investors were indeed wounded. We talked a good deal about another crowd fancy: conglomerate shares. We need not dwell on the advantages of having avoided the crowd in conglomerates.

So much for the "overdoing side" of the discussion. Let me turn to the other side.

The Underdoing of the Crowd

How to gain help from the *underdoing* of the crowd is as readily apparent as is the *overdoing*.

After the stock market has had a protracted slump, activities of the crowds become conspicuously unexciting. No one wants to buy anything, while the portfolio managers spend their time doing what they can to "mend their fences" and prepare for ensuing recovery and redemption of shares.

How can we employ these blue funks for profit? *Overdoing* shows up in newspaper headlines and financial publications, while *underdoing* bores readers and turns away those who would otherwise be enthusiastic about buying "a share in America."

Actually, of course, when the crowd is doing little or nothing — and the portfolio managers are culling and cultivating for the period ahead — contrarians prepare to do something about it.

One will ruminate over what future *demands* will be (when the revival sets in): what demands there will be for stocks as well as demands for products from industry. (The two dovetail, obviously.)

To me, the *underdoing of crowds* (who are concerned with investment and speculation) recommends to us conservative contrarians a policy of falling back on the old copybook maxim of depending on "the tried and true," (but not the "tired or through"). This applies to stocks as well as to individuals; indeed, applies to both.*

The sloganized emphasis in the "underdoing stage" is this: When everyone is thinking of doing little, the contrarian thinks seriously about doing more.

Someone will rise to say "yeah, maybe, but if you're too quick to go opposite to the do-nothings, you may find yourself caught in the tail-end of a down-draft that will put ten or twenty percent penalties on your purchase price."

I agree, but there is no avoidance of risk from timing. If one waits until he is sure that prices are headed up for a long bull market, stocks will have already advanced well up from their lows. You can never tell a bottom until you can look down on it! It is up to the investor to buy *values*, when the crowd has been in the underdoing stage, and not be frightened off by the inveterate bears.

---

* Perhaps we should remind ourselves that there is danger in thoughtless extrapolations. Because XYZ was a bonanza stock in the previous bull market does not necessarily mean you can count on its being a prime-mover in the next go-round. However, standard "growth" earners, whose products have growing markets, may safely be relied upon when "the psychosis of the panic has passed."

Following a severe slump in the stock market, gloom and bearishness persist for long periods, in relation to the extent of the prior fall and current news-developments. Naturally, one's contrary thoughtfulness takes in these factors when coming to a decision to act. The point is one has to act if he is to take advantage of the crowd's *underdoing.*

A final note: The crowd's do-nothing-sentiment means that the "dogs" which were popular in the overdoing days" will receive little or no attention for some time. Speculators and manipulators will let the dogs alone until their feel of the market tells them the crowd is getting ready again to try its luck at getting rich-without-working.

Meanwhile, sound, well-established companies, *with strong balance sheets*, and with expanding demands for their products, provide us contrarians with all we need in the way of receptacles for any excess reserves we are fortunate enough to have on hand.

This Ruminator believes there is valuable guidance to be had from the actions of the Crowd, both during overly-optimistic and heavily-pessimistic environments.

THE PERSUASION OF CROWDS

What We Need To Know About It

Let us look at crowd psychology from the viewpoint of the instigators, instead of from the side of the interrogators.

That is, in place of asking ourselves questions about what the Crowd is doing, suppose we inquire into what makes the Crowd do what it does, and why.

The inclusive word for it is persuasion, and a book you will find useful for details that I shan't have room for, is The Process of Persuasion, by Professor Clyde R. Miller (Crown Publishers, 1946).

The processes of persuasion are constantly before us: from the time we read the blurbs on the breakfast cereal boxes to the late news when we must suffer long night-caps of commercials. (I confess the commercials that seem to stretch out as bedtime nears has destroyed my interest in the evening news. I wonder how long the public will put up with (a) endless stale rerun programs, and (b) multiplicity of commercials that are forced upon us after the announcer has informed his captives that "we now return you to the program" — a decidedly sneaky and unethical practice, in my view.) Persuasion must lose some of its effectiveness when commercials reach the stage of boredom and disgust, but I have not noticed results of any tests, as I assume have been conducted.

I'll get off personal complaints and get back on our subject.

Persuasion covers the wide field of influences which induces action by people, whether it be to buy a given product or a basketfull of products; or to parade in front of the White House; or to buy a hot stock.

As Professor Miller explains, "once a custom (habit, fad or general desire) is established it means, in terms of persuasion, that you can persuade people in wholesale lots.

That is because all of us, to use a term now common in medicine and psychology, are creatures of 'conditioned reflex.' "

Conditioned reflexes are created by mass appeals of various types, from word-of-mouth to propaganda and publicity in the mass media. Such reflexes are established when you wish to gain distribution for a product, win political office, persuade the crowd to buy your shares (by publicizing how well your company is doing) or, in reverse, if you desire to defeat a public proposal or candidate for office.

Panics are created by "reflexes" that suddenly react to unexpected news, or to repeated happenings which finally "are too much to bear" and thus bring about the results that had been feared. We have witnessed this in recent years when international developments have suddenly taken turns for the worse — or when an unexpected (and unpopular) decision has been made, such as the widespread panic feelings created in 1970 when Cambodia was "invaded." Persistent declines in prices, in commodities or stocks, cause fear which in turn "persuade" traders and investors to sell, thereby increasing the chances of panicky conditions.

From this you grasp, I'm sure, some of the activities you need to get into to persuade the crowd to follow your wishes.

Appealing To The Crowd

If you intend to gain a following among the crowd, the first thing you must do is to determine what *appeals* to them. Your persuasive tactics have to be based upon what you know, or have found out, about the people in question. Do they know what you are after? Are they familiar with your product? — with you? — with your company? — in sum, with what it is you are trying to persuade them to think about, or take action in?

Let me inject that the contrarian, in analyzing persuasions of the crowd, makes an important distinction between thought and action. Where one may correctly "go opposite" to the actions of a crowd, he would not necessarily take action against the thoughts of the crowd, or group. A crowd may be persuaded of a given train of thought without being impelled into belief and action.

In planning to appeal to the crowd, therefore, one studies the possible reflexes that will aid in persuading the groups to accept his ideas. There are two kinds of reflex actions Professor Miller writes about. First is the "inborn or innate reflex," as when one yanks his hand off a hot stove he had thoughtlessly touched, or bats at a bee buzzing about his head.

The second form is an appeal that is acquired or has been taught. It is this latter type of conditioned reflexes that our studies of crowd psychology are largely concerned with.

Here we find where the powerful crowd-stimulants advocated years ago by Le Bon come into play: repetition and contagion.

A reflex is developed by repetition. Reflexes are created, for example, to launch a new product. In the present technological era there are numberless examples of "reflexes" which have had to be developed in order to get the public to accept the innovations, inventions, and original creations. Numerous products are still so "new" that they are comprehended by only a portion of the population of the advanced countries.

Gradually, as the advantages of the "new" over the "old" are recognized, the reflexes become conditioned to acceptance. During the process, an untold amount of effort is required. Education, propaganda, publicity and salesmanship must be extensively employed before people become so accustomed to the idea that they take to it naturally. Professor Miller calls these efforts "persuasion custom-made." He tells the story for instance, how people were "conditioned" to girls' smoking. I think you all know the story, and may remember how in initial attempts at persuasion, the advertisements pictured the boy-friend drawing heavily on a cigaret, which he blew in his fair partner's direction, upon which she remarked how pleasantly the smoke smelled! (Today we're under contrary conditioning!)

Four Devices In Persuasion Methods

I'll sum up our discussion with "four devices" as Professor Miller presents them in his book: for the acceptance or rejection of some person, group, product, program, policy, race or religion (which) is the fundamental aim of all persuasion. Four simple devices are used to achieve these aims." Let me put them down here as he does in his book:

> Acceptance or rejection of some person, group, product, program, policy, nation, race, or religion is the fundamental aim of all persuasion. Four simple devices are used to achieve either of these aims.

The Acceptance, or *Virtue*, Device — designed to cause us to accept by association with *good* words, symbols, acts.

The Rejection, or *Poison* Device — to cause us to reject by association with *bad* words, symbols, acts.

The Testimonial Device — to cause us to accept or reject by the testimony or evidence of persons considered *good, respectable, successful*, or inversely a *horrible example.*

The Together Device — to cause us to accept or reject by the application of any or all of the former devices applied through the pressure of group or mass emotion and action.

These four devices comprise, so to speak, the four sides of a square within which all persuasion is contained.

Once this is understood and digested you can subdivide or classify persuasion in any way that suits you best — you have it all.

We haven't space to enumerate a lot of examples, but many will come to your mind, I know. Under *virtue*, with Wall Street in mind, I think of better earnings' growth than anticipated; while for a *poison* device, the thought of "illiquidity" comes to mind; and for *testimonials*, there is the economic jawboning we receive from Washington.

It is important for us contrarians to get over on the other side of the fence occasionally. We have to know how "crowd opinions" are formed and arrived at — and acted upon. We cannot intelligently be contrary to something about which we know little of how it sprouted and became "persuasive."

WHAT'S THE USE OF IT ALL?

In protracted periods of discouragement one is inclined to say to himself, "What's the use of it all?" Yet, these are the periods when contrarians often make the most headway.

In these periods, also, contrarians find that opinions frequently have no pronounced one-sidedness. That is, no one seems to have hot ideas about jumping into things; people generally are more in a complaining mood.

You will not run across many extended periods of "doubt and dismay," if you check back through our economic history. In doing the Depression Vignettes in earlier booklets, I noted only a few stretched out terms when what's-the-use-of-it-all might well have been in countless minds.

The eras when this occurred were from 1836-1843, again in the 1870's, 1890's and 1930's. Unfortunately for cycle-minded readers, I do not sense any regular pattern in these eras. They were caused by the long, speculative build-ups which preceded them.

The severity of economic "doldrums- varies, of course. As we appear to be in another of those eras when one can get almost any opinion he wishes on the future, and when spirits are low, suppose we discuss it briefly. There are those who forecast times as severe and punishing as those mentioned above.

The Economics Of Carelessness

No better word to describe the prevailing mood of these long intervals occurs to me than *carelessness*. Indiscretion and imprudence brings them on. Lack of common sense and initiative prevail, until finally a revival of spirits results in revival of the economics.

In a minority of cases, *contrary thoughtfulness* provides a successful journey through the doubts and uncertainties.

A contrarian, if he is on the ball, does not say to himself, "What's the use of it all?" Instead he thinks, "How do I use it all to move ahead while others stall?"

So — it is up to us contrary-minded optimists to be about our business.

In the first place, are we deeply involved in an era of economic distress that will lead to a prolonged depression similar to those in past history? (For one, I can't see it.) How can we tell? What are the measurements?

There is one measurement which economists seldom use. They give little heed to the public psychology which prevails. Yet it is "how the people feel- which makes the cash registers ring and the time-clocks hum. When the sounds of activity decrease the contrarian speeds up his thinking apparatus.

A slowdown in economics spurs a pick-up in antithetics.*

And thus we develop, not carelessness, but carefulness; not a spirit of *give up*, but one of *make up* while the competition is lax. Did you ever stop to realize that it is easier to compete in the market place (regardless of your calling) when the traffic is low? For one thing, we can maneuver without getting clobbered by the Crowd.

---

* See Hegel's "triadic law," whereby a thinker moves from the general thesis to its opposite, the antitheses; from which he then draws a conclusion, or the synthesis. We employ contrariness in the same way: from popular opinions we derive contrary opinions, and from the latter we arrive at conclusions.

First, then, let us measure public psychology. It is not so much depressed, as lacking in fortitude (I refer to the dictionary sense of "firmness of spirit," which is surely lacking today). That doesn't call for a collapse.

Moreover, the times are suffering from the psychological effect of faulty forecasts. I am reminded of an acquaintance of some years back, Dr. L. Albert Hahn, internationally known economist of what was called "the Austrian School." Dr. Hahn placed great emphasis in his economic writings on the "unpredictability of predictions." I frequently quote his remark.

Before me is Dr. Hahn's book, *The Economics of Illusion,** a first-class book for contrarians. It was written as the 1940's were winding up, and the depression years were still in everybody's thoughts. He comments that "life has taught me that men, including economists, are influenced chiefly by their latest experience." He then added that until about the time he was writing everyone was still under the spell of deflation and had forgotten the preceding inflation.

> One more quote, which is applicable: "An economic policy that concentrates on artificially filling up an investment or spending gap rather than on fostering adjustments — and thus creating demand in a natural way — is doomed to fail in any severe crisis."

In trying to ferret out how a contrary approach will help us, we could do little better than to remember the idea expressed in *The Economics of Illusion.* In a planned society,

---

* Published by Squier Publishing Co., N.Y., 1949. Book is now out of print, I believe, but is probably available through the Fraser Publishing Co., Burlington, Vermont.

such illusions must appear. They cannot be avoided, because it is not possible to "plan" stability, or to program a society of full employment. It will be tried again, because the Congress passed a statute that says the President must keep everybody fully employed, but it takes more than a statute to make jobs: it takes expanding business.

Whenever the economy stumbles and speculation takes an old-fashioned prat-fall, you know from history what you have to do. Assuming a contrary attitude on your part (which has preserved you from disaster) you are now ready for the turn-about. In these protracted periods, there is no reason to rush into things.

When the sentiment of "doubt and dismay" obtains, the contrary program to follow is one of confidence and courage.

The economics of change requires that we give precedence to maneuverability. A Contrary Opinion policy calls for putting one's money and one's efforts where they will be least affected by change. A high proportion of "reserves- permits impartial and objective analysis of inflation prospects ahead.

THE PSYCHO STOCK MARKET

WHY NO SELLING CLIMAXES?

As we finished out the year 1970, the stock market was an interesting study in crowd psychology. Two "different" characteristics in the stock market's action put in their appearance . . . the absence of selling climaxes since the long fall in prices (from December, 1968 to May 1970), and secondly, the incidences of upside stampedes, under greatly increased volume of trading.

> What seems to have happened is a transformation: in place of selling climaxes that have in the past marked the end of down swings, the stock market has halted its declines, and then after girding itself, as a broad jumper does for a big leap, bounds forward with buy orders suddenly appearing almost in a frenzy.

From our studies in the Theory of Contrary Opinion we know that this type of fast change can only come from "crowd action." A most catching form of *contagion* evidently sweeps through the offices of investment managers, funds, speculators, and brokers' board rooms. Huge blocks, readied for purchase, plus untold numbers of smaller orders which had been decided upon ahead of time, apparently "hit the street" in as frantic a manner as is witnessed in selling climaxes.

> The buying rushes are not as thoughtless or as heedless as when the Crowd tosses stocks overboard in selling panics. I venture this distinction because *plans for buy orders, in such quantities*, have of necessity been under study for some length of time. Panicky selling is often done without reflection (shortage of funds may be a factor) whereas buying stampedes arise from Crowd activation of prior planning.

From the rather short period of time since "upside stampedes" have been so frequent and conspicuous we cannot be too sure of interpretations. However, I believe when the statistical studies of orders finally come out (if they do), we shall find that the "public," whose buying and selling Wall Street has always belittled, has broken down into two spheres: (1) Those who have ceased trading on their own and now have their money in Mutual Funds, and (2) the minority who continue in their own careful way. (And, believe it or not, are probably more often right than wrong in their investments. They don't panic, in selling or buying.)

If this supposition is correct, we may more and more witness the great volume swings on the upside — as funds and speculators jump aboard when they sense a move starting; while relatively moderate volume will occur when the market is settling into a bottom area. Indeed, a "series of bottoms" may be the development of the future, in place of "climax bottoms" traders and analysts have always looked for.

IN THE FIELD OF PSYCHOLOGY

As I have often remarked, a valuable fringe benefit of writing these publications is the correspondence from readers — and the extremely helpful ideas which are sent to me.

Crowd psychology is the basis for the Theory of Contrary Opinion, a study of which I have endeavored to foster over the years.*

* May I again say that it is most pleasing to me that the contrary theory is widely accepted in business and financial *thinking* circles as a useful and workable tool in decision-making. The coined word, *contrarian* is commonly noted in financial commentaries. The salutation "Dear Contrarian," has greeted readers of our Letters since way back in the 'Forties. Although not yet in the dictionaries, I'll wager the word soon will be.

When I receive a letter which touches on the question of mass psychology, or upon peoples' reactions to events and crises, I snap to attention.

Recently, a professional psychologist wrote a letter that I must share with you, as it suggests a future of real importance for contrary ruminating. Let me quote his closing words, and then I'll give you the gist of his thought:

> "Perhaps one day this (further study) will help provide ground for the integration of psychological and economic factors in coming up with a more and more effective psychological tool to help make decisions in the business environment. One that will utilize more and more reason and empirical evidence to support its concepts."

After remarking that my theory of Contrary Opinions has much in common with his views of human behavior, he quotes a philosopher in the First Century, as having stated the central thesis:

> "Men are disturbed not by things, but by the views which they take of them." — Epictetus

I have set that off by itself, because as in so many brilliant maxims, one has to digest it. My friend, the doctor of psychology (PhD, etc), says he holds to an approach known as "rational-emotive psychology," which is essentially the interpretation of the Epictetus axiom.

We, too, have always held that *emotion* headed the list of traits that make the contrary opinion theory workable. Let me quote again from the description given in Dr. S's letter:

> Putting the Epictetus maxim in A-B-C terms, we get this theory of behavior:

"A" refers to an event, and "C" indicates reactions to the event (usually stated as feeling). This leaves the key factor, designated by "B."

Explanation is in order. The B factor is what one *tells himself* about the event in question, but does not take seriously. The usual story is that such-and-such event upsets one, makes him angry, etc. In other words, that A caused the reaction C.

This is challenged by Dr. S. He says, "No. You made yourself angry, at C, by what *you told yourself* (B) — which is in your own head!"

We are told to "search for alternatives." Seek evidence to support or not support our own beliefs, our "emotiveness." Dr. S. refers to this writer's looking for alternative interpretations of events in business and non-business environment, which, interestingly, he thinks is kin to his studies.

THE "CROWD" IN 1970

When The Nation Panicked And Everybody Went Haywire

In years to come, commentators will look back at the virulent spring fever, of 1970, and relate how the stock market, Wall Street, and people everywhere panicked.

Everyone went haywire and lost their sense of balance because, as Wilfred Trotter wrote in *Instincts of the Herd in Peace and War*, individuals are responsive to impulses coming from the herd.

The impulse of the invasion of Cambodia carried people away. It was an instance of "crowd participation" that equals any mob activity you will find in the history books.

"The individual will treat the herd as his normal environment," wrote Trotter. "The impulse to be in and always remain with the herd will have the strongest instinctive weight. Anything which tends to separate him from his fellows, as soon as it becomes perceptible as such, will be strongly resisted."

In this book originally published, in 1916, in London, the author points to the gregarious instincts that are especially noticeable in wartime. We all noticed the extraordinary reactions to the war in Vietnam, that worsened steadily.

Wars cause people of all types to lose their individuality at times. Emotion takes over, and self control vanishes. The Cambodian panic was a particularly severe one. Reactions to it were dramatically reflected in the stock market —which is always the mirror of people's emotions. Stocks were tossed on the market without any connection whatever with the developments in Cambodia, or with the intrinsic values of the securities. It was as if thousands of stockholders suddenly were determined to discard valuable properties in an attitude of "this will show them."

Why a person gets any satisfaction in taking a loss to register a point, I'll never know. Trotter explains it, in part, when he says that "primitive instincts normally vestigial or dormant are roused into activity by the stress of war, and that there is a process of rejuvenation of 'lower' instincts at the expense of the `higher'."

When you think back, even with the advantage of many months' hindsight, it is impossible to bring back the "feelings" of the period. Don't you find it so?

This writer has just turned back to see what he wrote in May, 1970 about the Cambodia incursion.

> "Contrary-minded as I am, nevertheless I failed completely to foresee the saddest contrariety in American history: namely, the abject abdication of so much our country has stood for. • . . Mob psychology is revealed in all manner of activities, including stock prices. A revolt in sentiment can mean a rout in the stock market. .. . Present levels are unreasonable, answerable only by mass psychology . . . etc."

Intelligent managers of money cried out, as stock prices fell, that "illiquidity" would cause failures of banks and businesses. Mild-mannered people became panic-stricken, and there were immense sales of stocks at panic levels. Interestingly enough, however, there never was the "selling climax" technicians waited for. Instead, nerves were brought under control and in place of selling climaxes we witnessed a series of buying stampedes in the months that followed.

Students of contrary opinion have in the year 1970 one of the most significant eras to study and analyze. Just as we refer to manias of former times — from the Stock Market panic of 1929 on back to the Tulip Mania in Holland — so students will refer to the Cambodian Panic of May, 1970.

PERTAINING TO THE LAWS OF CONNECTIVE THOUGHT

Thirty-five years ago I (somewhat conceitedly) wrote an essay purporting to show others how a writer puts mental images into words that will cause the reader to *think* (and to act, if the writing were for advertising or for some advisory counsel).

A key to the notion was the creation of "a continuing train of thought" in one's presentation. It is this creation of a *theme* that keeps the reader interested.

As I reviewed the piece which I had long past forgotten it occurred to me that I had not touched on one or two of the ideas in some time. As they are relevant" to contrary-opinion thinking I'll make use of them here. I'll work the ideas around to fit the reader, as well as the writer.

If we are (a) to fight shy of preconceived opinions, (b) restrain pride-of-opinion, (c) avoid distracting interests, and (d) cure that distaste some of us have for "coming to a decision,- we must have a plan to check our thoughts.

To present mental images and trains-of-thought to overcome these and other inhibitions requires an understanding of human nature. May I stress that it not only requires an understanding but a great curiosity about why human nature acts as it does! Why do we go off half-cocked, why do we grasp at tips in the stock market, why are we mental copycats?

> Opinions are transient — seldom constant — and are continually swayed by hopes, fears and *anticipations.* Today's trends of thought and feeling become tomorrow's trends of business and finance. Thus economic factors must be deciphered for their effect on human emotions and not simply weighed in the balance of cold logic.

This is a guide-line the Ruminator has kept before him since his early days.

It is necessary to have a theme in mind before one starts to write, so the reader will have it in mind when he reads. Call it a running topic, or a hook to hang your ideas on, or what you will, but without a theme both writer and reader are likely to get off the line-of-thought and never get back. The density in some writings on economics turns readers away.

Association Of Ideas Helpful

Professor William James long ago formulated "ideas for the association of objects" which are helpful for understandable reading:

> Any object not interesting in itself may become interesting through becoming associated with an object in which an interest already exists. (Substitute *idea* or *thought* for the word *object* and the application to contrary-opinion ruminations be- comes clear.)
>
> ". . . things not interesting in their own right borrow an interest (from things that *are* of interest to the reader).
>
> "The odd circumstance is that the borrowing does not impoverish the source, the objects taken together being more interesting perhaps than the originally interesting portion was by itself."

The association-of-ideas method of presenting contrary-opinion ideas, or any themes connected with thinking and writing on socio-economic subjects, has become a habit of mine, as readers have undoubtedly noticed. However, a point I want to make here is that this method is not any more valuable for the writer than for the reader. That is, the reader has the task of digesting the writer's thoughts and of *recasting* the association-of-ideas when he feels the writer has got off the track.

There are four "laws" of connective thought, which apply to this theory of association-of-ideas and to our continuing study of contrary opinions. These laws may be stated as follows:

1. The law of Inherent Connection;
2. The law of Opposition (of Contrary Opinion);
3. The law of External Connection;
4. The law of Similarity.

These laws (and I must apologize for having no recollection if they were original with me; I suspect they were suggested by my readings in books by James, Robinson, Le Bon or other popular psychologists) — these laws are of course applicable to the Theory of Contrary Opinion. Back in those days I was getting more and more involved in the problems of Crowd Psychology and the application to economics. I believe the initial idea of a "letter of contrary opinions" came to me in 1936 or 1937 when the stock market went through gyrations that had everybody, including the experts, scratching their heads to learn what happened. (The drop in prices in 1937 was the swiftest ever recorded.)

Application To The Present

Coming down to the present era, I think you will agree that the foregoing is even more timely today than in former frustrating periods.

Opinions are formulated, discarded, altered, and copied more speedily and carelessly than in former times. This is caused by the speed of communication, and especially the "persuasiveness" of television commentaries, speeches, and panels — coupled with the dramatic presentation of news, often slanted in accordance with what to the producer is the significant or "newsy" side of the happening in question.

> How many of us stop to realize that many of the scenes presented to us in our "evening news" would never have been staged (on the street or in some hall) unless the "actors" knew a television camera was there to pick up the story? So we have to put the light of contraryism on television as well as on the views presented to us by commentators. We look for the "connective thoughts."

A final note. Another development that has come to the surface in recent years is the *variety* of Crowds that now seem more apparent than formerly. The conspicuous example is found in stock-market circles. As I have often remarked, there are now not only the "crowd" commonly thought of as being "the public," but the groups who, for instance, manage investment funds. "The law of similarity" frequently shows up in their activities. Then there are the large numbers of "economic dissertators" whose views appear in bulletins, letters, in the press and over the air. . . . often strikingly alike in their opinions.

We contrarians, because of the stress of the era, also have the difficult mental task of keeping up with the changes in world opinion. One need only mention China for illustration. Who would have forecast that a friendly entente with the Peoples Republic of China would be given even a moment's thought while signs about "the running dogs of U.S. imperialism" were still posted on China's streets?

We surely have to be "contrary" to keep up with what's going on!

WHY BE A CONTRARIAN?

The August, 1971, economic pronouncement from President Nixon gave an opening again to write on one of the most important advantages in the Theory of Contrary Opinion.

It reminds us to restrain our "dogmas." We learn not to be cocksure and dogmatic about things we really have no way of knowing how they will turn out. To repeat an old favorite of mine, we quit trying to predict the unpredictable. (See next page.)

A kindred contrarian, Edmund A. Opitz (of the Foundation for Economic Education), sent me a quotation from Burzon's book, *Science: The Glorious Entertainment,* that puts a scientific twist on Contrary Opinion that I find enlightening. Burzon calls it "The Method of Contradiction." He says it is one of several approaches various scientists have used.

> "It consists in assuming the opposite of the established doctrine and seeing where this will lead. To uphold the negative requires reasons, which require new facts, which require the invention of new experiences. It is a risky method, for doctrines do not get established without the support of innumerable observations. But when it succeeds it means a 'revolution'."

References such as the foregoing add to my faith that we are on the correct path in being contrary thinkers. At least we do think upon occasion, be- cause as I have so often remarked, you cannot conjure up contrary notions unless you have thought about a subject. Contrary opinions do not come from thin air; they require a lot of oxygen to come alive.

Contrary Opinions Should Come Ahead Of The Dogmas

Let's say that you have a "fixation" on the trend of the stock market. We'll assume that this is at an imaginary time, not in the present or recent past.

You *know* which way it is going. But, having heard about the theory of contrary opinion you decide you'd better be contrary. What do you do about your fixation? Well, I'll tell you what some folks do who think they are contrarians. They look around and try to uncover a contrary slant that will support their previous set opinion. You can usually find some idea, somewhere, that will back up any notion you have. Preconceived opinions are mind-closers.

Obviously, that is not the way to go about contrary analysis. Note above, Professor Burzon warned that "to uphold the negative requires reasons. ..." If you have preconceived opinions, you will find it almost impossible to accept new facts and observations that will allow you to check the contrary viewpoints and perhaps change your opinion altogether.

As I ventured to write at the time of the Nixon televised program, August 15, 1971, "don't rush to be contrary." What I was aiming at was that contrary opinions take time to collect and ruminate over. There was bound to be an impetuous mass reaction to the message (as there was). Time was needed to see things in a contrary light.

Those who had been dogmatic in their views, prior to the economic program outlined by the President, immediately sought angles that bolstered their previous ideas.

Experienced contrarians, on the other hand, recognized that the President's plans were far more comprehensive, more encompassing, than anyone had envisioned. That is to say, the message was a surprise; indeed, a shock. Therefore the immediate responses through-out the world could not be considered contrarily and thought out until enough time had elapsed for emotions to subside and repercussions to occur.

I used the expression that "immediate contrary opinions are likely to be anybody's opinions."

Stock markets always give us quick reactions to news. It was educational, how in the Nixon "package plan," markets reacted in different countries. The Japanese "Dow-Jones average" collapsed while the Yankee D/J went wild on the upside.

As comments appeared in the press and in bulletins of advisory services, it was informative to note how a few commentators quickly recognized the "changes" which were sure to follow; while others clung to their former views, refusing to see that anything had changed.

I am sure readers will agree that you cannot put the economy in a straight-jacket, compel citizens to refrain from price or wage increases, and additionally close the gates at Fort Knox (where supposedly we have nine or ten billions in gold), without experiencing a changed economic pattern.

So, let us seek numerous observations, in our contrary searching, in order that we may have sound reasons for "going opposite" — and, even more importantly, in order that we may avoid becoming dogmatic and unchangeable in our views.

THE SHORT, VERSUS THE LONG, RUN

We ventured in August, 1971, it was time to be contrary to gloom and discouragement. I suggested we were at another juncture when the future would shift for the better.

While long-range judgments are always "subject to events," one may arrive at a short-run guess, if he approaches it from the standpoint of mass psychology. By short-run, I am thinking in terms of six months to a year. The long-run is an "unknown."

The Nixon program shocked the country from its lethargy and dejection. It unquestionably raised people's spirits and hopes.

NOW TURN BACK 68 YEARS

Few can recall the period prior to the financial panic of 1907. The year 1906 was extraordinary, from the standpoint of business and financial activity. Monetary worries became as much of a concern among bankers and businessmen, during the 1906 boom, as has been the case in our present and recent experience. It helps our perspectives to note an occasional press report from earlier times. The following appeared in an editorial, January 5, 1906, in *The Press,* Philadelphia.

An "Inelastic Currency"

"The artificial character of the current advance of securities becomes apparent when the market breaks as it did yesterday on the N.Y. Stock Exchange under a speech like that of Mr. Jacob H. Schiff before the New York Chamber of Commerce.

"The misfortune is that such a break in a speculative market, caused by a speech on the inelasticity of our present currency, will deepen the public conviction that a more elastic currency is wanted for speculators. Nothing could be less true. From the present system business suffers worse than speculation. . . .

The editorial goes on to point out that "serious trouble" was in store unless something were done to curb the reckless stock gambling and ridiculous looseness in the money markets (where interest rates on stock-exchange call money rose as high as 125% and fell as obliquely).

By the autumn of the following year, the Wall Street panic had brought the matter acutely before the country.

PUT YOUR MONEY WHERE YOUR MOUTH IS

This inelegant expression from the race track and the prize ring has its analogy to our Theory of Contrary Opinion.

There is constant chatter about what's going to happen. Numerous people like to vent their views and say what they are going to do about it. Yet, more times than not their money is nowhere near their mouths. You might call such talk "fleeting opinions."

We contrarians have to separate these fleeting opinions from those which appear to have some substance. What it comes down to, if I may say it again, is that actions count more than words.

However, the words have to be considered. Opinions, as they "congregate" and become general, are effective in causing action.

The period following the 1971 "freeze," was illustrative, I think, of a condition that is most confusing when we are trying to think straight "by going opposite."

Let me use the stock market for the discussion. Stock prices give an outlet for both thought and action.

This question is sometimes asked: Does action always follow thought? Of course not. Everyone thinks of a thousand things to do, of action to take, only a fraction of which is ever attempted.

Accordingly, a contrarian — when deciding what to be contrary about — must attempt to figure out whether what appears to be a *consensus* is being accompanied by action, or is merely "mouthings."

Additionally, we have to estimate if those whose opinions and actions we're checking, are likely to change their minds. People shift rapidly at times.

Sudden, unexpected news-events, of striking significance, will cause overwhelming activity in the stock market. The August 15th, 1971, announcement of the "freeze" was an example.

We witnessed action without thought. Then, as "second thoughts" accumulated, contrary action became evident. What happened was that a burst of stock-buying without thought was followed by a dragged-out period of selling as thoughts turned to doubt and apprehension. And the selling picked up momentum as worries spread over Phase 2.

During the same period, other confusing actions and opinions were present. Various polls of people known to be interested in the stock market reflected a bullish rather than a bearish attitude. Moreover, the bi-weekly check of advisory services conducted by Investors Research of Larchmont, N.Y., revealed an unusually heavy proportion of bullish over bearish forecasts.

"Actions Speak Louder Than Words"

Thus we witnessed a replay of the old proverb: actions speak louder than words. However, there is a fallacy in the proverb, too. Words, translated into widely scattered opinions, frequently are purposely released to effect a desired "crowd reaction." Then it is called Propaganda.

The contrary analysis, therefore, of a given popular view must determine if the actions are louder than the words, or if the words are creating an entirely opposite result from the apparent action.

Albert Jay Nock, a boon companion (in his books) to contrarians, referred in one of his essays* to Jeremy Bentham, who invented the expression "imposter-terms." Bentham, it seems, left an unfinished work, on Fallacies. He put them in a general category, Nock tells us, of "fallacies of confusion." Suppose we take space to reprint how Bentham observed that imposter-terms are employed:

---

* See Nock's *Free Speech and Plain Language*, (William Morrow and Co., 1937). A collection of essays that appeared in the *Atlantic Monthly* and *Harper's Magazine*, in the early 1930's. Jeremy Bentham was an English philosopher: 1742-1832. His ideas were often "contrary."

1. A fact or circumstance which, under its proper name and seen in its true colors, would be object of censure, and which therefore it is necessary to disguise.

2. An appelative which the sophist employs to conceal what would be deemed offensive, or even to bespeak a degree of favour for it by the aid of some happier accessory.

3. The object of their use is to cause by means of the artifice, that to be taken for true which isn't true. . . .

In our contrary approach we broaden the idea of imposter-terms to include opinions which are not necessarily untruthful, or purposely misleading, but merely someone's, or some group's prejudices or predictions.

Politicians, for example, conceal their offensive remarks, without being outside the truth. A prominent banker may be extremely bearish, we'll say, but does not wish to frighten or worry the banks' customers, or the public. He therefore disguises his pessimistic feelings, yet puts them in such a way that his sophisticated clients will "get the message."

NO TIME TO GIVE UP

I recently replied to an inquiry by saying that "things could not be more depressing in the news, so I shall sleep well tonight."

It was not to be a smart-aleck, but merely to attempt in this way to express the theory of Contrary Opinion.

Every so often, in a free-enterprise system, we run into slumps in the stock market when there seems to be no bottom in sight, or any end to the persistant selling of stocks. It reminds old-timers of 1937, when liquidation of shares had all of us observers standing open-mouthed as stocks seemed to pour out of cracks in the walls. Such movements pass quickly, but are very painful while they last.

These are times when we call upon Contrary Courage and Contrary Confidence. We know that when stocks are thrown overboard thoughtlessly that the recovery trend in the future will be equally impressive. The recovery will be painful only to those who assume that Wall Street is washed-up, that stocks will never again reach 1000 in the famous Dow-Jones industrial stock index, for instance.

In historic financial eras it has been significant how, when conditions were slumping that, under the pall of discouragement, economics were righting themselves underneath for the ensuing revival and recovery.

Advisors And Brokers Thrive On Bull Markets

A writer in Business Week, in May, 1968, depicted the excitement then commonplace over the growth in "computered advice." The article was titled, in fact, "Computers Spew Out Hot Advice." As the writer pointed out, "the innuendos (he referred to advertisements and claims then being touted for advice via computers), to some unsophisticated investors, may suggest a magic — or at least scientifically infallible — method of pinpointing stocks to buy, to sell or to hold."

As with all "crowd fevers," we know from hindsight that computerized advice has not been any more accurate than any other advice. In the final analysis it is the judgment behind the data fed the computer, as well as the judgment behind one's note-pad, that determines whether advice is good or bad.

So it was when the tide turned, advices then emanating from gloomy quarters would have had us give up all hope, sell stocks, go short of the market, and prepare for Armageddon. This advice, too, was only as good as the judgment of the forecasters issuing the advice. Such forecasts reached the opposite pole from the computerized hot tips of 1968 — and were accorded, by contrarians, the same contrary opinion with which the excesses of 1968 were greeted by experienced contrarians.

GREGARIOUS MAN

As we reach the end of this collection of contrarisms, it is well again to talk about "gregarious man." All of us know about him. However, as the herd instinct seems to grow ever more "enveloping" in the area of socio-economics and stock markets, we may give it final attention.

The word comes from the Latin, gregarius, meaning herd. It is an excellent word for our studies in contrary opinion, because it immediately presents a mental image of animals, birds, or people, gathered together or perhaps rushing about, as in a stampede.

Readers have noted that in my comments about the stock market, I have used the word "stampede" in reference to various fast rises in stock prices. In recent years there has developed a powerful "herd" of stock-market operators — or portfolio managers — who definitely reflect the gregarious man.

Man has always liked to gather with his fellow human beings. In former times, in this country as well as abroad, the saloon was the favorite meeting place where kindred souls could swap stories while quaffing an inexpensive glass of beer. They still do, of course, but a persuasive new medium has been introduced in the form of television. Nowadays, both men and women sit glued to their TVs and thereupon become members of the largest flock ever assembled. While separated physically, they are convened mentally, and react to herd instincts as they would if assembled in a hall.

True, the TV listener is not a member of a mob that may rush off and throw rocks, but he is susceptible to what psychologists term the "*suggestibility*" of the crowd, even though he may be sitting alone in his living room.

The suggestibility can endure, and build up, in individuals, the feeling that they wish to join *the herd* and get into action.

Instincts Of The Herd

Readers will recall that I have mentioned a book by Wilfred Trotter, which was published in 1916, titled *Instincts of the Herd in Peace and War*. The first world war was the instigator of the author's studies.

Let me quote again from the author's preface, as it gives us a viewpoint on the herd instinct that may need rewinding.

> The general purpose of this book is to suggest that the science of psychology is not the mass of dreary and indefinite generalities of which it sometimes seems made up; to suggest that, especially when studied in relation to other branches of biology, it is capable of becoming a guide in the actual affairs of life and of giving an understanding of the human mind such as may enable us in a practical and useful way to foretell some of the course of human behavior.

Students of Contrary Opinion will agree, I think, that we have found the study of crowd psychology to be extraordinarily useful in judging the possible course of human behavior in politico-economic and in market trends.

Unquestionably, it is useful as the activities of crowds are affected by the instincts of the herd. I believe it is correct to suggest that crowds are *increasingly* affected, because of the enhanced pressures of opinions and ideas that constantly confront people everywhere. The psychology of modern communication has yet to be thoroughly understood, but without doubt it augments the actions and reactions of the crowd.

Characteristics Of Gregarious Man

The cardinal quality of the herd, asserts Trotter, "is homogeneity. It is clear that the great advantage of the social habit is to enable large numbers to act as one. . .

We might say, in thinking of the astonishing activities of crowds and mobs over the recent years, that the herd instinct has been a great *disadvantage*. I am sure many times that you have wished, as I have, that it had taken days and weeks for news to reach us about the Vietnam war, as thereby the shock of bad news would have been dulled by time as well as by distance. Surely, in times prior to instant communication, there was not the flash effect of news. In old newspapers I go over occasionally, much of the news concerning events other than local was set in very small type (perhaps half this size you are reading) and often over on the back page of the paper. I have found Civil War news treated in this manner.

Homogeneity denotes "sensitiveness to the behavior of (one's) fellows." How plainly we note this in stock-market news and resulting activities.

IN CONCLUSION

And so we come to the end of another "collection of thoughts and suggestions" on the author's Theory of Contrary Opinion.

An earlier book, *The Art of Contrary Thinking*, by the same publisher, was first issued 20 years ago, in 1954 (and was expanded through five editions).

In the intervening time the Theory has had wide acceptance, so I can only say to the reader, "try it out and prove it to yourself."

AFTERWORD
Reflections on my Father, Humphrey B. Neill
The Vermont Ruminator and Father of the Theory of Contrary Opinion
By Albert R. Neill

Thinking Vermonters "ruminate." Like a cow chewing her cud, the Vermonter turns thoughts over and over in his or her mind, not rushing to judgment. Can this be translated into an investment philosophy? My father published a series of essays on his ruminations of the contrary approach to market trends in 1975, now presented in a revised edition of his publication popular among thinking investors, *The Ruminator.*

My father never attained the riches that he advised others to attain, but he lived a comfortable life, providing for his family. He was conservative in his views (a traditionalist believing in small government, fiscal responsibility, a balanced budget and a laissez faire approach to economics), yet he was progressive in making choices in life and in forging new and creative ways to think and act in the world around him, and in discourse and writing. He pursued vigorously and enthusiastically his interests in books, history, human events, photography (both as an award-winning amateur and professional), the country life in Vermont, and even a short stint as a chicken farmer.

He was a patriot and firmly defended the tenets of American democracy, individualism, and a free market economy. At the age of 21 he joined the Army and served in the last horse-drawn artillery unit under General John J. (Blackjack) Pershing that chased Pancho Villa back into Mexico in the ill-fated Mexican Campaign, and then later in the American Expeditionary Force in France in WW I, where he received a field commission to 2nd lieutenant. On December 7, 1941 he sent a telegram to Secretary of War Stimson volunteering his services to fight the Axis. Too old for active service, he worked energetically on the home front in World War II selling war bonds and served as our county's chairman.

Recently, rummaging through my father's papers I came across a time-faded file with the notation: "Notes – Rough Drafts of Possible Autobio." Inside there was a roughly typed manuscript entitled *Introductory – Chapter I: Through 45 Years of Contrary Opinion,* written about 1975, a year or two before his death in June, 1977. He wrote: "I became imbued with the spirit and practicality of 'contrary opinion' in 1929. It was a wildly fluctuating time in the stock market all year, climaxed by a smashing end of America's most expansive speculative era to that time." At that time, he recounts he was serving as business manager of a division of Brookmire Economic Service* which led him into writing which "might be tagged a financial philosophy," and started a small house organ for Brookmire, entitled, *If, As and When.* It quickly took on the sub-title of *Passing Thoughts and Reflections on Human Nature in Finance.* He notes that this was a writing activity that continued some 45 years to that very day (in 1975).

My father cut his teeth in Wall Street in the 1920s with various market advisory services which followed the market daily, researched stocks and offered recommendations for clients. He later moved his office to our home in Larchmont where he maintained a huge wall chart that stretched around three sides of his large 3rd floor studio where he plotted daily the high, low and close of the Dow Jones Averages—industrials, utilities and transportation.

He called himself a "point and figure man," and with his intimate knowledge of market movements put himself in the position to author a well-received volume, *Tape Reading and Market Tactics* (1931). Yet even in these pages you can detect his leanings toward what later became his basis for the Theory of Contrary Opinion: the realization that the stock market is essentially a stage for human interaction, and prices are established by human decision-making as much as by technical indicators.

Then came the Crash and the Great Depression and Humphrey's studies of the human element and crowd psychology led him to formulate the Theory of Contrary Opinion. As the decade of the thirties came to a close, our family moved to Vermont to occupy a spacious 16-room homestead on the outskirts of the village of Saxtons River that had been in the family since 1828. My dad was the fourth generation in the same home, and now I am the fifth. Following, for some 30 years he wrote and published the *Neill Letters of Contrary Opinion* from his vantage point in "contrary country," Vermont. (In the early years the letter was mimeographed, and then later reproduced on an offset printing press. During those mimeograph years, I can recall witnessing my father roll a stencil into his Royal Standard typewriter and type the first and final copy to mount on the mimeograph drum: clearly he had been ruminating about what he had to say for some time before this exercise.) In 1954 he published a small book which attained widespread circulation (including an edition in Japanese), *The Art of Contrary Thinking* (Caxton Press). In 1975 he produced *The Ruminator: A Collection of Thoughts and Suggestions on Contrary Thinking.* Both books are now being re-released by Caxton Press in entirely new and updated 21st Century editions, and in "e-book" formats, including these musings about the original author and an extensive Introduction reflecting on the historical significance of The Theory of Contrary Opinion, and relating these musings to current trends and developments in the marketplace by Tim Vanech, Investment Advisor.

Along the way, the theory of contrary opinion and its author gained public notoriety in a number of ways. In the May 25, 1959 issue, *Time* magazine featured an article on Nicolas Darvas, a Hungarian-born professional dancer, entitled *Pas de Dough* explaining how he had amassed a fortune of over $2,000,000 in the stock market while continuing his dancing career. Among other items of interest, Darvas studied the market backstage between his appearances and was quoted as saying there were two books that he re-read each week, one of them being Humphrey Neill's *Tape Reading and Market Tactics.* The book was then out-of-print and prices shot up for the few copies in the second-hand book market. My father contacted the publisher, B. C. Forbes, who was not in a position to rush out a new edition, but kindly gave the rights to my father and had their office staff type the entire text on mimeograph stencils. My father then issued a "special edition" in mimeographed form with an updated foreword and worksheets for use by the reader and marketed it through his newsletter and limited advertising. Two copies remain in our Vermont library today. On the copyright page he passed on this note of sagacity:

> A requisite for a successful speculator is a 'money mind' ... those of us without this tantalizing quality of mind will have to be satisfied with a more gradual accumulation of a share of this world's goods, and be content with making friends, enjoying the beauties of life and reading books for pleasure and erudition.

And while no records seem to exist, he wrote in a scrapbook carefully kept by my mother, "We sold thousands of these."

In 1967, Edward Johnson II, founder of Fidelity Investments, launched the *Contrafund*, naming it after my father. On the 10th anniversary of the fund in the May 20, 1977 edition of the *Wall Street Journal,* Fidelity ran an ad featuring a photo of my father deep in thought with a young man alongside who queried, "Mr. Neill, on behalf of Fidelity I'd like to acknowledge your theories that led to the development of *Contrafund.* But tell us, sir, what have you been up to lately?" To whom my father replied: "Ruminating, young man, ruminating." Yes, the *Contrafund* was targeted at investors who wanted to benefit from carefully examined contra trends utilized to identify undervalued stocks and, if you will, managers that "ruminated" before making investment decisions. Today, the *Contrafund* has over $60Bn in assets.

In his later years, my dad's eyesight started to fail. I bought him a magnifying light so he could continue to read. Then I flew off to Greece for a long-term work assignment. He purchased a typewriter with jumbo letters (about font size 30 on our computers today). The last note I received from him the letters ran right off the page, so frustrating for a man of letters, who contributed with passion to the market's lexicon—words like "contrary," "ruminate" and others. He passed away shortly after that. On June 6, 1977 he attended a meeting of the public library board of trustees, came home, had supper and fell into an eternal sleep in his favorite chair in the living room. He was 82 years old. On cold winter nights in the old homestead in my imagination I can still hear the *tap, tap, tap* of his Royal Standard as he interprets the day's events from a contrary point-of-view.

Saxtons River, Vermont
May 2010

Al Neill spent much of his lifetime living and working in Greece, Egypt and the Near East, and Sub-Saharan Africa in health and development. He was in Ghana when he received word of his beloved father's passing. He is now retired and living with his wife and son in the old family homestead in Saxtons River, Vermont.